MINI

ICELAND

How to download your Free eBook

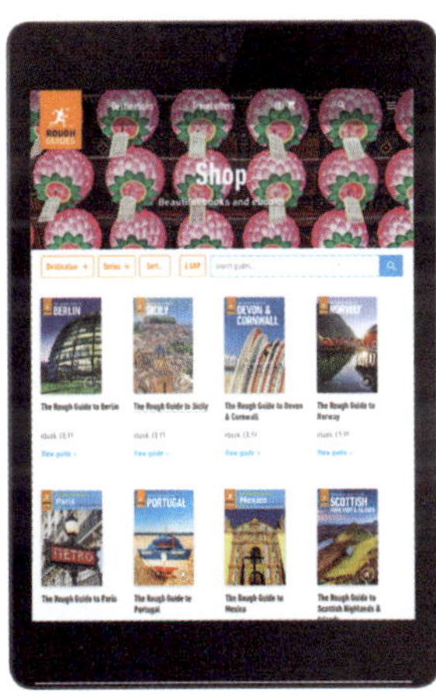

1. Visit **www.roughguides.com/free-ebook** or scan the **QR code** opposite

2. Enter the code **iceland310**

3. Follow the simple step-by-step instructions

For troubleshooting contact: mail@roughguides.com

Contents

Introduction

Few places on Earth can match the raw and intense beauty of Iceland. Both fiery and cold, forbidding and inviting, it is a place of dramatic extremes, home to immense ice fields, bubbling mud pools, colossal waterfalls and hot springs. Although Iceland has a long, rich cultural history, it is the land itself, sculpted by the forces of nature into a unique, ever-changing landscape, that tells the country's true story.

Underground Drama

In geological terms, Iceland is a mere baby, composed of some of the youngest rocks on earth and still being formed. Over the centuries, eruptions have spewed vast fields of lava across the island's surface and projected choking clouds of ash high into the air, blocking out the sunlight and blighting crops. In 2010, the ash cloud from a volcanic eruption under Eyjafjallajökull glacier paralysed Europe's

WHAT'S NEW

Iceland's not the kind of place to constantly indulge in grand construction projects, although notable additions in recent years include the Sky Lagoon, a Reykjavík alternative to the Blue Lagoon: it opened in 2021 and was expanded in 2024 to include a traditional Icelandic 'turf house' wellness section. The Sky Lagoon does not boast the cobalt blue water of its famous counterpart, but is less touristy and has a beautiful setting, carved out of sea cliffs. The capital also saw the opening, in 2023, of Edda, a research centre for Icelandic studies which is hosting the World in Words exhibition throughout 2025, a collection of sagas and other historic manuscripts. Nearby, the government is planning to open a new National Gallery, which will be close to the Harpa Centre. The Akranes Folk Museum in western Iceland, meanwhile, saw the opening in 2024 of the new A Local View exhibition, dedicated to the work of painters from the area.

air traffic for six days; in 2023 and 2024, a series of eruptions near Grindavík led to the repeated closure of the Blue Lagoon. Every day there are thousands of minor earthquakes and shocks, most of which are only detectable by seismologists.

The presence of so much natural energy just below ground makes it possible

NOTES

Iceland straddles the North Atlantic Ridge, where two of the tectonic plates making up the Earth's surface are slowly drifting apart. The country is widening at a rate of roughly 2cm (0.8in) annually. Along this fault line, from the northeast to the southwest, earthquakes and volcanic activity are commonplace.

Dettifoss in Vatnajökull National Park

not just to see the awesome power of nature, but to feel, hear and smell it. The limitless reserves of geothermal energy that have produced such a varied terrain also supply heat and power to Iceland's homes, and the 'rotten egg' smell of sulphur is unmistakable whenever you turn on a hot tap. Dams across fast-flowing glacial rivers provide the nation with more than enough hydroelectrically generated power to meet its needs.

The abundant hot water not only heats homes and offices: in winter it is piped under pavements in the centre of Reykjavík to melt away the snow and ice. All year round it contributes to the social life of the Icelanders, filling outdoor swimming pools, where people meet to take a little exercise or just to chat in the hot tubs and steam rooms.

Pollution-Free Land

For Icelanders, keeping their landscape clean and pollution-free is a top priority. It is with justifiable pride that they boast that the water from any stream or non-glacial river is drinkable, due to the lack of heavy industry. Even in the capital, Reykjavík, the air is bitingly clean and light pollution is minimal – when the Northern Lights are in full flow, they can be seen from the city. You won't

THE ICELANDIC HORSE

Horses have been used for transport and farming in Iceland for over 1,000 years. The country's isolation and a ban on importing new horses to keep out disease mean that its horse population is remarkably pure. Icelandic horses are relatively small but extremely tough and they can handle the rugged terrain with ease. They are found in a wide variety of colours and are respected worldwide for their intelligence, stamina and speed. The Icelandic horse has a unique gait, known as a *tölt* – a kind of running walk with a gentle flowing movement that makes for a very smooth and comfortable ride.

see rubbish tipped at the wayside here, nor will you encounter widespread burning of fossil fuels. There are several foreign aluminium smelters in the country, drawn by Iceland's clean energy; however, the industry has been facing a lack of demand and their future remains uncertain.

Making friends on a farm

High Standard of Living

Iceland is a European nation, although it remains outside the European Union mainly to protect its economically vital fishing grounds. It has strong social institutions and a well-funded welfare system. Few Icelanders are conspicuously rich, but there's little urban poverty, and the standard of living throughout the country is high.

Geographically equal in size to England, Iceland has just 394,000 inhabitants, two-thirds of whom live in the capital and its sprawling suburbs. Icelanders have a powerful respect for nature and know they can never expect to control it or have it all to themselves. The shy Arctic fox and the reindeer are rarely seen, but sheep are plentiful, and horses are widely kept. Millions of seabirds flock to the country's cliff tops and coastal meadows to nest during the bright summer months, while offshore, whales, dolphins and seals are abundant in some of the cleanest waters on earth.

Icelanders make the most of the many benefits of their extraordinary environment, spending as much time as possible outdoors

WHEN TO GO

Icelandic weather is notoriously unpredictable. In summer there's a fair chance of bright and sunny days, and temperatures can be mild, but good weather is interspersed with wet and misty spells when days can get chilly. Many museums and attractions outside Reykjavík are open only from late May to early September, and it's at these times, too, that buses run their fullest schedules. Although almost all of Iceland lies south of the Arctic Circle and therefore doesn't experience a true midnight sun, nights are light from mid-May to early August across the country; in the north, the sun never fully sets during June. In winter temperatures fluctuate at 7–8°C either side of freezing point and daylight is limited to a few hours – in Reykjavík, sunrise isn't until almost 11am in December; the sun is already sinking slowly back towards the horizon after 1pm. That said, between September and January the Aurora Borealis or Northern Lights can often be seen throughout the country, and this is also the time of year to explore the ice caves of Vatnajökull.

during the long summer days. Walking, climbing and horseriding are popular pursuits, and, as the importance of tourism has grown, so too has the number of companies offering snowmobiling on the glaciers, hiking adventures in the interior and whale-watching off the coast.

Reykjavík

Dominated by brightly painted buildings and a massive central church, Reykjavík is a lively place. Here a modern, cosmopolitan city has evolved beneath the snow-capped mountains. The population may be small, but it is clear from the cafés, restaurants and nightclubs that this is a place where people know how to have a good time. However, the scene starts late, and the often eye-watering prices for alcohol and a decent meal force many locals to get their eating and a fair bit of their drinking done at home before they venture out.

WHAT'S IN A NAME

According to tradition, Iceland owes its name to a Viking adventurer who chanced upon it around AD870. After spending a long, hard winter watching his cattle die from the bitter cold and lack of good grazing, he climbed a mountain only to see the fjord choked with drift ice. Wholly disenchanted, he named the place Ísland, literally 'ice land', and promptly departed for the positively balmy climes of his native Norway. Four years later one of his compatriots returned and started the first proper settlement at a place he called Reykjavík, or 'smoky bay', from *reykr* ('smoke') and *vík* ('bay'). His inspiration was the plumes of steam rising from nearby thermal springs.

Skaftafell ice cave

Outside the capital, some towns, notably Akureyri in the north, share some of Reykjavík's energy, but most are happy not even to try. The smaller towns are quiet, compact and neat, often no more than a cluster of colourful houses around a church or shop. The pace of life is slow, and the sense of community strong.

Hot Springs and Outdoor Baths

Since the late 1970s the country's only major road, a vast circular route around the coast, has linked village to town and countryside to capital. Most communities are found on or near the ring road, a short distance from the sea, where the land is at its flattest and most fertile. This narrow coastal plain, the only truly habitable part of the country, makes up just one-fifth of Iceland's total area.

Fortunately, much of the most impressive scenery is easily accessible from the ring road. The site of the original Geysir, which gave

SUSTAINABLE TRAVEL

Iceland is uniquely placed when it comes to sustainability, blessed as it is with a volcanic furnace which provides the country with a bottomless source of geothermal power. At the time of writing, around 85 percent of the country's energy supply was provided by domestically produced renewable sources, which is the highest proportion in the world. You'll feel the benefit of this not only in the heating of your hotel or apartment, but in the country's famous geothermal swimming pools, a dip in which is a pillar not only of a trip to Iceland, but of Icelandic society itself. The country also uses geothermally heated greenhouses to grow tomatoes and bananas; you can experience this side of Icelandic agriculture at the Friðheimar farm and restaurant, near Reykholt. Most buses in Rekjyavík are already electric, and many car hire companies offer electric options; there are plenty of charging points dotted around the country. The government also encourages visitors and locals to forgo bottled water for the tap water, which is some of the cleanest in the world.

Geothermal power station

its name to all geysers around the world, is close to the capital, as is the best outdoor bath on the planet, the Blue Lagoon. The mighty Vatnajökull glacier, the largest in Europe at 8,400 sq km (3,200 sq miles), reaches down to the sea across the southeast of the country.

To the north, Jökulsárgljúfur (now part of the Vatnajökull National Park) is not only an impressive tongue-twister, even by Icelandic standards, but also home to Europe's largest, most powerful waterfall, Dettifoss, which plummets into the canyon below amid clouds of rainbow-coloured spray. In the north and west, the coastline is splintered by craggy fjords and the sheer granite sides of flat tabletop mountains. Further inland, wide valleys rise towards the barren upland plateaux that constitute the interior. This is Europe's last wilderness, a wide expanse of bleak grey lava desert fringed by volcanoes, glaciers and mountaintops.

10 Things not to miss

1 **ÞÓRSMÖRK**
One of Iceland's most dramatic wilderness areas. See page 66.

2 **HEIMAEY**
A quintessential Icelandic fishing port with an attractive harbour. See page 63.

3 **REYKJAVÍK**
Iceland's vibrant capital has many cultural attractions. See page 33.

4 **GEYSIR**
No visit is complete without seeing Iceland's hot springs. See page 52.

5 **GOÐAFOSS**
Witness the power of these staggering falls. See page 85.

6 **BLUE LAGOON**
Bathe in the naturally heated, therapeutic waters. See page 48.

7 **LAKE MÝVATN**
A bird-watcher's paradise surrounded by volcanic peaks. See page 85

8 **NORTHERN LIGHTS**
The most breathtaking lightshow on earth. See page 8.

9 **JÖKULSÁRLÓN**
This spectacular iceberg-studded lagoon is out of this world. See page 71.

10 **WHALE-WATCHING**
Spot one of these majestic creatures off Húsavik. See page 81.

A perfect day in Reykjavik

9.30AM

Pancakes and coffee. Start the day with breakfast at your hotel or head to the retro-style café, Grái Kötturinn, on Hverfisgata 16a, for pancakes with bacon and syrup, and a coffee.

11AM

Shoreline stroll. Take a morning walk past the glittering Harpa concert hall to the harbour area. You could take in a whale-watching trip from one of the boats moored here. Check out Icelandic pop art at the Hafnarhús gallery (see page 41) and admire Mt Esja across the bay.

12.30PM

Lobster stop. Stop for a bowl of lobster soup and an Icelandic beer at Sægreifinn fish shack, on Geirsgata 8.

1.30PM

Reykjavík's heart. Take a walk through Austurvöllur square, the city's traditional heart, where you'll find the statue of Jón Sigurðsson, Parliament House and, adjacent, Reykjavík's modest cathedral, the Dómkirkjan. Slip past the City Hall to see the birdlife on Tjörnin pond.

2PM

Heritage walk. Walk down Reykjavík's oldest street, Aðalstræti, and look in at the city's most modern heritage museum, the Settlement Exhibition Reykjavík 871±2, for some Icelandic history.

3PM

Retail therapy. Head to Reykjavík's main shopping street, Laugavegur, for exclusive, cutting-edge fashion labels alongside vintage clothes (Spúútnik at 28b is particularly good for this). Branching off diagonally, Skólavörðustígur is lined with beautiful art and design shops.

5PM

Steam and soak. Time to recover from shopping and sightseeing at one of Reykjavík's many geothermal pools. The most central is Sundhöllin, on Barónsstígur. The pool is indoor, with outdoor hot pots to relax and gossip in – the perfect way to get ready for the night ahead.

8PM

Fine dining. There are many excellent restaurants in the city centre. Two options are Sjávargrillið at Skólavörðustígur 14 (see page 123) and Dill at Laugavegur 59 (see page 122), a moodily lit, first-floor restaurant.

10PM

On the town. Austurstræti is a good place to start: grab a well-made cocktail at the Jungle Bar (no. 9, on the 2nd floor). Laugavegur and the surrounding streets are packed with iconic bars and clubs, such as Kaldi Bar (Laugavegur 20b) and Kaffibarinn (Bergstaðastræti 1). If you're up for a pint and darts, just a few blocks away is Bastard Brew and Food (Vegamótastígur 4), with their own and other locally brewed beers on tap.

Classic Iceland

DAY ONE

Morning: Enter the volcanic realm. Enjoy a hearty breakfast in Reykjavík to fuel you up for your outdoor adventures. Café Loki is a beloved local institution where the menu includes traditional ingredients – try the skyr (Icelandic yoghurt) French toast. Then, depart the capital for Iceland's famous Golden Circle (see page 49), with the first stop the remarkable Thingvellir National Park (Þingvellir in Icelandic). This volcanic landscape was the site of Iceland's first parliament, and is the only place on Earth where you can walk (and snorkel) in between two tectonic plates.

Afternoon: Geyser-gazing. Continue along the Golden Circle to Geysir, the natural feature which gave its name to geysers worldwide. Nowadays, eruptions of Geysir itself are infrequent, but nearby Strokkur reliably shoots water and steam into the air every 5–10 minutes. Carry on the road for ten minutes or so to Gullfoss, an awesome cataract which is one of Iceland's mightiest waterfalls.

Evening: Culinary curiosities. You're not too far from Reykjavík, so spend the evening enjoying the comforts of the capital. Try a traditional dinner at Islenskí Barinn (see page 122), where delicacies include grilled puffin and – if you dare – the infamous *hákarl* (fermented Greenland shark). Then, dive into the city's famously vibrant nightlife; dozens of clubs and bars are clustered around the Laugavegur thoroughfare.

DAY TWO

Morning: Waterfalls and beaches. Set out early this morning from Reykjavík for Seljalandsfoss, a magnificent set of falls 1.5 hours from Reykjavík which tumbles over a cave, offering the rare opportunity to walk directly behind a waterfall. Continue to the coastal town of Vík, a further hour away. Vík is famed for its jet-black volcanic sand beach, and for the obsidian rock formations, known as Reynisdrangar, which grasp upwards through the roiling waves – a stunning photographic negative of a place.

Afternoon: Frozen world. After a packed lunch, jump back in the car and make for the glacial wilds of Vatnajökull National Park. Vatnajökull is Europe's second largest ice cap, and is home to magnificent ice caves which can be explored each winter before they melt and then form again, taking unique shape each time. During the summer, ice hikes and snowmobile tours are alternative ways to explore this magnificent ice kingdom.

Evening: Aurora-hunting. Watch the sunset over the remarkable Jökulsárlón Glacier Lagoon, an icy lake floating with icebergs, and then drive back to Reykjavík. If the night is clear and dark, embark on a Northern Lights-spotting bus tour from the capital; otherwise, treat yourself to dinner at one of the city's finest restaurants, such as the classy Sjávargrillið, where the seafood menu includes an acclaimed lobster soup.

Hidden Iceland

DAY ONE: AKUREYRI

Flower power. Fly into Iceland's second-largest town (population: 19,219), renowned for its sunny summer days and thriving bar and restaurant scene. Take advantage of its comforts at restaurants like Rub 23 (see page 124), and stock up on supplies in the shops of Hafnarstræti, while making sure to tick off attractions like the Lystigarðurinn (Botanical Gardens), home to some 7,000 flower species, and the Akureyrarkirkja, the town's impressive church.

DAY TWO: HÚSAVÍK

Whales and puffins. Just an hour's drive from Akureyri is the bayside fishing town of Húsavík. Whale watching is on everybody's list of must-dos in Iceland, and the expertly run tours from Húsavík offer virtually guaranteed sightings. Another option from Húsavík during breeding season (June–August) is a boat trip to see puffins on the islands of Lundey and Flatey. The fascinating and often controversial history of Icelandic whaling is also documented at the Húsavík Whale Museum.

DAY THREE: LAKE MÝVATN

Waterworld. A further 45 minutes by road south of Húsavík is Lake Mývatn, one of Iceland's most restful spots. This being Iceland, there is a proliferation of geological oddities here, from bubbling mud pools to steam vents, which cluster around a beautiful lake teeming with birdlife. Twitchers can spot harlequin ducks, whooper swans and greylag geese, among dozens of other species. Take the time while in the area to also explore Dettifoss, the country's most powerful waterfall.

DAY FOUR: THE INTERIOR

High drama. Venture into Iceland's Highlands to witness some truly awe-inspiring scenery: from glaciers to lava deserts, this is where Iceland's true wilderness adventures lie. The roads are mostly unpaved, so many visitors choose to visit on a tour with a driver, but it's perfectly possible to self-drive as long as you rent a sturdy 4x4. Once upon a time, only intrepid campers would venture into the Highlands overnight, but nowadays there are plush, luxurious places you can stay, such as the Highland Base hotel, set beside steaming fumaroles.

DAY FIVE: THORSMORK

Verdant to volcanic. On the southern edge of the Highlands lies Thórsmörk ('The Valley of Thor'), one of the country's most beautiful corners. Hemmed in by soaring green mountains which plunge to a black, volcanic valley floor, this is a place of meandering rivers, wildflower meadows and fantastic hiking through woodlands of dwarf birch – as close to a forest as you get in Iceland. This is also the final terminus of the Laugavegur Trail, which, if you have the time, is Iceland's finest hike: 34 miles to Thórsmörk from the rhyolite mountains of Landmannalaugar Nature Reserve.

History

While elsewhere in Europe, civilisations, empires and dynasties came and went, Iceland remained uninhabited and undiscovered. It wasn't until the 8th century AD that Irish monks became the first people known to have set foot on the island, relishing its solitude. They left no physical trace behind either (though some crosses in south Iceland appear to be stylistically related to crosses from western Scotland), nor, being all men, any new generation. Within 100 years the peace they had enjoyed was no longer: the Vikings were coming. Much of Iceland's history was chronicled within a few hundred years of the events happening. The *Landnámabók* (Book of Settlements), probably written in the 12th century, describes in detail the first permanent inhabitants. The sagas, dramatic fictional tales of early Iceland penned 100 years later, add a lot more colour to the story.

The First Settlers

The country's first settlers were Norwegians, thought to have been escaping political persecution and economic hardship at home. They found Iceland by accident, having already colonised parts of both Scotland and the Faroe Islands. The official 'First Settler' was Ingólfur Arnarson, who enjoyed his first winter so much that in 874 he went to fetch his extended family and friends to come and join him. His foster brother Hjörleifur fared less well in the new land: his Irish slaves

NOTES

Although many Icelanders can trace their families back to the early settlers, family names do not exist. Instead, children absorb their father's first name into their own. A man named Eiríkur Gúðbrandsson might, for example, have a son named Leifur Eiríksson and a daughter named Þórdís Eiríksdóttir.

mutinied and murdered him, fleeing to the Westman Islands after committing their crime. However, there was no indigenous population for the colonisers to evict or butcher, and the biggest threat they faced was from the elements.

These first Icelanders established farms in the rather more hospitable parts of the country, and within 60 years there were approximately 25,000 people living around the coast. Some basic laws were already in place: a man could claim as much land as he could light bonfires around in one day, so long as each new fire could be seen from the previous one. Women could have as much land as a heifer could walk around in a day. Inevitably disputes broke out, which the local chieftains had to resolve. When they failed, there could be bloody battles.

Viking relics at the National Museum of Iceland

The First Parliament

In AD 930 the chieftains got together and agreed on a relatively democratic system of government. A Commonwealth was established, with a national assembly or *Alþingi* meeting for two weeks every summer at Þingvellir. Here, new laws would be agreed and infringements of old laws settled by a system of regional courts. The worst punishment was to be declared an outlaw and banished from the country.

The system wasn't perfect, and there were still some bloody battles – these were, after all, the descendants of Vikings, who valued courage and honour above all else. Nonetheless this period is now considered to have been a Golden Age, the Saga Age, full of great heroes and wise men.

From Pagans to Christians

Soon, however, things were to change dramatically. Christianity had spread to northern Europe, and the zealous, if bloodthirsty, King Ólafur Tryggvason of Norway wanted Iceland for the new religion too. When his missionaries encountered resistance in the late 10th century he was all for butchering the entire population until the Icelandic chieftain Gizur the White promised to have another go by more peaceful means. Fortunately the lawspeaker, who presided over the Alþingi, was at that time the widely respected Þorgeir. He persuaded both sides to agree to accept his decision in advance and then went off to meditate. He came back and announced that Iceland would become Christian, although pagans could continue to practise their beliefs in private.

Bishoprics, monasteries and schools quickly followed, and books were soon being written for the first time. As a sign of their independence, the writers chose to do their work in Icelandic, not Latin. There were so few foreign influences in the centuries to come that the language they used is almost identical to the Icelandic spoken today.

All was not well in the land, however, and Iceland was about to enter its Dark Age. The Hekla volcano outside Reykjavík erupted in 1104, burying nearby farms; over-grazing and soil erosion from excessive tree-felling further reduced the amount of viable land. At the same time the church became greedy and, by imposing tithes, it split the formerly egalitarian society. Some chiefs, who were given church lands or made into senior clergy, found themselves increasingly rich and powerful. Before long, the most important families started fighting for supremacy. The Alþingi, which had relied on people voluntarily accepting its authority, was now powerless to respond.

Civil War and Black Death

Soon the country was in a state of civil war, which only ended when Norway took sovereignty to help maintain order in 1262. Iceland kept many of its old laws, but 700 years of foreign domination had begun.

Revolts and skirmishes continued, while nature also took its toll. Long, harsh winters destroyed farm animals and crops, yet more eruptions covered parts of the country in ash, and the Black Death arrived in Iceland, laying waste to almost a third of the population.

Those Icelanders still living were too busy struggling to survive to notice that Denmark had taken over the Norwegian throne and was therefore their new master. But the Danes took little interest in their new acquisition, despite it possessing something the rest of Europe suddenly wanted: cod. Fishing brought new wealth to coastal landowners, but it brought new trouble, too.

English and German adventurers started appearing offshore, fighting among

Statue of Ingólfur Arnarson, Iceland's official 'First Settler'

THE SAGAS

Between the 12th and 15th centuries, some of the great stories the Icelanders had previously passed on from generation to generation were written down. Collectively known as The Sagas (literally 'things told'), they are universally acknowledged as one of the world's most important bodies of medieval literature. Scholars argue about how accurate they are, but for complex characters and subtle storytelling they are unbeatable. Families are torn apart by feuds, cursed heroes are doomed to exile, formidable men and women meet their ends defiant. The sagas are written in an unemotional style that makes the brutal fates of many of their characters even more shocking. The manuscripts were collected for posterity by Árni Magnússon (1663–1730) and taken off to Copenhagen for safety, but most were then lost in a terrible fire. Árni himself braved the flames to rescue some of them. The surviving Sagas weren't returned to Iceland until long after Independence. Perhaps wary of their troubled history, the authorities in Reykjavík keep the majority under lock and key, although some are on display at the Culture House.

themselves, indulging in piracy and trying to control the trade in dried cod. The English got the upper hand, and this became known as the English Century.

The Danes eventually realised that they were losing out financially. When Denmark tried to ban the English from the country, the latter killed the governor and started bringing in their canons. By 1532, however, the tide had turned, and the English leader was killed in renewed fighting with Germany. However, from then on England let the Danes and the Germans fight among themselves and turned their attentions elsewhere.

The Reformation

The Church was still a dominant force in the early 16th century, and when Scandinavia turned Lutheran during the 1530s it was inevitable that Iceland would soon follow suit. By the middle of the 16th century, the transition had taken place, and Protestant Reformation had been well and truly imposed on an unwilling Icelandic population.

By this time, Denmark was gaining increased political authority over Iceland, and eventually complete control of the country was passed to Copenhagen. From 1602 all of Iceland's trade had to pass by law through a small group of Danish firms, a move that effectively bankrupted the country. Smallpox then wiped out almost a third of the impoverished population, and, just when it seemed as if matters could not get any worse, thousands more citizens were killed in 1783–4 by massive eruptions that poisoned almost the

Jón Sigurðsson, leader of the independence movement

NOTES

Jón Sigurðsson (1811–69) is a great hero to Icelanders. A scholar and MP, he agitated for independence from Denmark. He helped to achieve limited home rule, but died in 1879, long before sovereignty was restored in 1918.

entire country and caused widespread famine. Denmark considered evacuating the whole surviving population, but decided instead to relax the trading laws a little and give the country a chance to recover.

As it did so, educated Icelanders looked to continental Europe and saw democracy stirring in once-powerful monarchies. Jónas Hallgrímsson, a poet, and Jón Sigurðsson (see box), a historian, started a fledgling independence movement. By 1843 they succeeded in getting the Alþingi revived as a consultative assembly – it had been suspended since 1800. A decade later, trade was freed up completely. Slowly, prosperity started to return.

In 1874, Denmark, now a constitutional monarchy, returned full legislative powers to the Alþingi. Several substantial changes came into play: the tithe system was abolished, schooling became compulsory, and the fishing industry was allowed to grow and prosper. By 1900, Iceland had its own political parties. In 1904 it was granted Home Rule and in 1918 gained independence, though it kept the Danish king as monarch.

War and Peace

Iceland, now trading with England and Germany, was neutral in World War I, although the Great Depression of the 1930s hit its growing economy hard. In World War II, control of the North Atlantic was a key strategic objective, and first Britain, then the United States, landed forces in Iceland. Denmark was invaded by Germany in 1940: left to its own devices, Iceland dissolved its union with Denmark entirely and declared itself a republic in 1944.

Iceland's strategic location made the new government feel nervous as the Cold War gripped the western world. In response, it joined the UN and then NATO. Still, the decision to allow US forces to return to their wartime bases in 1951 provoked riots in Reykjavík.

When Iceland next went to war, however, it was with a fellow NATO country, Britain. The so-called Cod Wars, that came and went for 30 years after 1952, were no more than a bit of naval muscle flexing. Britain objected to successive extensions to Iceland's territorial waters and sent patrol boats to protect its trawlers. In 1975, it ordered its frigates to ram Icelandic coastguard ships, which had been cutting the cables of British trawlers. Eventually, in 1982, Iceland got its way, and 325km (200-mile) limits became the norm worldwide.

Since the last quarter of the 20th century, the country has been increasingly outward looking, attracting foreign businesses and visitors. In 1986, the world's media descended on Reykjavík for a nuclear summit between presidents Reagan and Gorbachev.

A young Icelander

Although the European Union's stringent fisheries policy has deterred Iceland from joining that group, all argument was rendered void after the 2008 worldwide economic crisis, prompting Iceland to apply for EU membership in the hopes of greater financial security. However, it was

Watching a volcanic eruption on the Reykjanes peninsula

never a popular move, and the 2013 election to power of a centre-right coalition government was widely interpreted as a big 'no' to EU membership. Two years later, the new government formally withdrew Iceland's application for EU membership. When Europe was engulfed by the Covid-19 pandemic in 2020, Iceland's response was characteristically swift and efficient, resulting in widespread testing and vaccination, and comparatively few deaths.

Iceland's economy is diversifying, ending its reliance on fishing to focus on hydroelectric power and its booming tourism industry. Iceland looks to the future as a proud and independent nation, happy to cooperate with the world community – but reluctant to be dictated to by it.

Chronology

c.8th century AD Irish monks start to settle on 'Thule'.

c.870 A Norwegian, Hrafna-Flóki, tries to settle in the West Fjords, calling the land *Ísland* (Iceland).

874 Ingólfur Arnarson and his family and friends settle on Iceland.

1000 Christianity is adopted as Iceland's official religion.

13th–14th centuries Norway and Denmark feud over ruling of Iceland.

1389 Huge eruption of Mt Hekla, followed by the Black Death.

15th century England and Germany battle to control the cod trade.
1662–1854 Trade monopoly with Denmark.
1783 Eruption of Lakagígar craters poisons land and leads to famine.
1800 Danish King abolishes the Alþingi; it is reinstated in 1843.
1874 Denmark gives the Alþingi autonomy over domestic affairs.
1918 Iceland made a sovereign state under the Danish monarch.
1944 Independence from Denmark declared on 17 June.
1952–75 Cod Wars (1952, 1958, 1972, 1975) with the UK.
1955 Halldór Laxness wins the Nobel Prize for Literature.
1963 Surtsey Island created by an underwater volcanic eruption.
1973 Volcanic eruption on Heimaey Island.
1986 Nuclear summit between Reagan and Gorbachev held in Reykjavík.
1994 Iceland enters the European Economic Area.
2000 Mt Hekla eruption in February; earthquakes in June.
2006 Iceland resumes commercial whaling.
2010 Eyjafjallajökull erupts, bringing Europe's air traffic to a standstill.
2015 Iceland's application for EU membership is withdrawn; the Bárðarbunga volcano erupts.
2016 Historian Guðni Thorlacius Jóhannesson becomes Iceland's youngest president. Prime Minister Sigmundur Davíð Gunnlaugsson resigns.
2020 Hildur Guðnadóttir becomes the first Icelander to win an Oscar for her music to The Joker. The Covid-19 pandemic sweeps Iceland, causing restrictive measures to be put in place to contain the virus.
2021 The Covid-19 vaccine sees a high rate of uptake in Iceland.
2023 A series of volcanic eruptions begins near Grindavík, continuing into 2024 and resulting in widespread evacuations and closures of sites.
2024 A new government takes office in Iceland, comprising a coalition of the Social Democratic Alliance, the Liberal Reform Party and the People's Party.
2025 Iceland joins the United Nations Human Rights Council.

Kirkjufellsfoss, on the north side of the Snaefellsnes Peninsula

Places

Iceland is one of the world's most spectacular destinations, with vast empty landscapes illuminated by sparkling, clear, sub-arctic air and cosy fishing villages sheltering from Atlantic storms beneath gargantuan cliffs. It is a paradise for anyone with a love of nature and the great outdoors, lent a surreal edge by its lunar landscape and the ever-restless tectonic activity below.

Visitors range from the experienced adventure traveller in search of new challenges to those on a two- or three-day stop-over between Europe and North America. Whether you come for several weeks or just a few days, there will be no shortage of things to see and do. Iceland's infrastructure is well designed and efficient, making independent travel almost as easy as taking one of the many commercial tours and excursions.

Iceland works almost exclusively in English, so a lack of Icelandic is not usually a problem. Facilities are constantly improving, and the number of people visiting Iceland means there is usually a range of options when it comes to choosing tours or means of transport.

Reykjavík

Highlights

- **Hallgrímskirkja and Vicinity**, see page 35
- **Central Shopping Area**, see page 37
- **The Government District**, see page 38
- **The Harbour Area**, see page 41
- **Western Reykjavík**, see page 42
- **Eastern Reykjavík**, see page 44
- **Viðey and Lundey**, see page 46
- **The Outskirts**, see page 47

Stopping to admire the view at Tjörnin lake

Most visitors start and end their trip in **Reykjavík ❶**, and many are surprised by how small and insubstantial it can seem. There are virtually no high-rise buildings, certainly there are no skyscrapers, and the use of corrugated iron and timber in many of the buildings makes them look almost temporary. In fact, the building materials and layout of the city are very practical and, like everything else in Iceland, are designed with the elements in mind.

Reykjavík is a destination in its own right. Over a third of the country's population live in the capital, where they enjoy fresh air and a magnificent location between the

NOTES

Reykjavík is the world's most northerly capital city, at 64.08°N, and at 21.55°W it is Europe's most westerly capital.

bay and the mountains and glaciers of the interior. Apart from a few major roads around the edge of town, the streets are narrow and sometimes steep. The city's energetic and distinctive cultural scene is a constant source of fascination, yet it retains a certain slow pace and almost rustic charm that makes it unique among the world's capitals. Moreover, everything you will want to see is either within walking distance or a short bus or taxi ride away.

Hallgrímskirkja and Vicinity

The central importance of the massive **Hallgrímskirkja** Ⓐ (off Bergþórugata; www.hallgrimskirkja.is; free, charge to climb tower) is quickly revealed on the drive into the capital across the lava fields from the airport to the south. The church is so enormous that it not only dominates the skyline, it reduces everything else to virtual insignificance. The eye is constantly drawn back to it and its bizarre shape resembling a rocket ready for lift-off. The church is the most obvious place to begin a visit to Reykjavík, and you will almost certainly approach it up Skólavörðustígur. As you head uphill on this street, take time to look in the windows of the enticing galleries and bijoux boutiques, reflecting how much artistic talent such a small country has produced.

Statue of Leifur Eiríksson

Reykjavík rooftops

A lift runs up the Hallgrímskirkja's 73 metre (240ft) tower – with a few stairs at the end – from where you are rewarded with the best view of Reykjavík from the viewing platform. Designed by Guðjón Samúelsson, it is a monument not only to Christ, but also to Reykjavík's belief that being a small city need not limit its ambitions. The church itself is very bare, as befits its Lutheran status, and there is not much to see except the magnificent **organ**, which is 15 metres (50ft) high and has more than 5,000 pipes.

Just outside the church is a **statue of Leifur Eiríksson**, Iceland's greatest adventurer, who reached America long before Christopher Columbus. The statue, which is by Alexander Stirling Calder, was a gift from the US government to mark the Icelandic parliament's 1,000th anniversary in 1930.

Nearby is a museum dedicated to Einar Jónsson (1874–1954), one of Iceland's greatest modern exponents of sculpture and the master of symbolism and epic: the **Safn Einars Jónssonar** **B** (Einar Jónsson Museum, Njarðargata; www.lej.is; charge). Jónsson was virtually a recluse towards the end of his life and many of the 100 or so pieces exhibited here are dark and sombre in character. At the back of the building, on Freyjugata, the small sculpture garden is open year-round.

Central Shopping Area

Returning to the bottom of Skólavörðustígur brings you to Reykjavík's main shopping street, **Laugavegur**. The name translates literally as 'Hot Spring Road', and it means what it says – it was once the path taken by townspeople who were going to do their washing in the hot pools in Laugardalur (see page 45). Today, thanks to the city's unique geothermal heating system, the same source is used to help to keep pavements and car parks ice-free in winter, using underground water piped up from the Laugarnes boreholes. The street is home to a mixture of international shops, local stores, cafés, bars, restaurants and hotels… plus the world's only penis collection at the **Icelandic Phallological Museum** **C** (Laugavegur 116; http://phallus.is; charge). On display are over 200 specimens from almost every mammal found in Iceland or in its waters; four human donors have bequeathed their members to the museum.

Higher-minded souls will find greater pleasure at **Þjóðmenningarhúsið** **D** (Culture House, Hverfisgata 15; www.culturehouse.is; charge). The key exhibit is a fascinating collection of medieval manuscripts containing rare sagas and *eddas* full of details of life in Iceland and elsewhere in northern Europe from the time of the Vikings onwards.

Reykjavík's Rainbow Road

There is also a collection of memorabilia from the struggle for independence. It is all housed in a splendid building, opened in 1909, that was initially intended for the National Library.

The city square of Austurvöllur

The Government District

At the western end of the main shopping street, after its name changes to Bankastræti, is the government district – **Government House** is not open to the public but is nonetheless well worth a look from the outside. It is one of the oldest houses in the country, dating from 1761 when it was built as a prison. It now houses the offices of the Prime Minister.

Across Hverfisgata, standing on a hillock, is an imposing **statue of Ingólfur Arnarson**, the first settler, looking out over the Atlantic. Behind him is the National Theatre and to his right are some of the government ministries.

The Icelandic parliament has only 63 members, so its headquarters, **Alþingishúsið** Ⓔ (not open to the public), is a well-proportioned but unassuming grey basalt mansion (1881) on Austurvöllur. In between 2008–16, archaeological digs around the building have unearthed the first Viking-Age industrial site found in Iceland: an iron smithy and fish- and wool-processing facilities were once located here. When parliament is sitting, its debates can be observed from the public gallery; but they are, of course, in Icelandic.

Alongside Alþingishúsið is Reykjavík's stone and corrugated iron Lutheran cathedral, **Dómkirkjan** F (http://domkirkjan.is; free), built in 1785, which has a rather plain facade, and a trim, galleried interior with arched windows that bathe the place in light.

The grassy square in front of the parliament, **Austurvöllur**, is popular with picnickers in summer. One of the great campaigners for independence keeps a watchful eye over proceedings: the **statue of Jón Sigurðsson,** known as *The Pride of Iceland,* rises above the square. A couple of streets away is another square, **Lækjartorg,** where you'll find one of the two city bus stations.

The most tangible signs of Iceland's Viking settlement can be seen at the **Reykjavík 871±2 Settlement Exhibition** G (Landnámssýningin; https://borgarsogusafn.is/en/adalstraeti-en; charge) at Aðalstræti 16. Here you will find the remains of an oval-shaped Viking-Age farmhouse just below the current street level, along with one of the country's most impressive and imaginative exhibitions. The city's main tourist office is at the end of the road.

Just to the west, on the banks of **Tjörnin** H, a city-centre lake, is **Raðhús** I (Reykjavík City Hall, corner of Tjarnargata and Vonarstræti; free). This modern glass-and-concrete construction, designed to link the people with their politicians and the city buildings with the lake, is a key example of 20th-century Icelandic

REYKJAVÍK CITY CARD

Consider investing in a Reykjavík City Card, which can be purchased from tourist offices, bus terminals, museums, the City Hall Information Desk and many hotels at a cost of ISK5,500 for 24 hours, ISK7,700 for 48 hours and ISK9,500 for 72 hours. The card gives access to a great selection of museums and galleries, the Family Park and Zoo and all of the city's swimming pools. It also allows unlimited free travel on the city buses and a ferry trip to Viðey Island, plus discounts in some shops and restaurants and on some tours.

architecture. It has a café, an exhibition space and a large relief map of Iceland.

Alongside the lake is **Listasafn Íslands** J (National Gallery of Iceland, Fríkirkjuvegur 7; www.listasafn.is; charge). This small gallery has a fine permanent collection of work by Icelandic artists, including the country's first professional painter Ásgrímur Jónsson (1876–1958). There is a café on the first floor with internet access. A couple of blocks away is a very different kind of visual experience, the **Icelandic Punk Museum** K (Bankastræti 2; www.facebook.com/Bankastraeti0; charge). This tiny but packed exhibition is located in the old public toilets in Bankastræti Zero. The exhibition tells the story of the local punk and new wave movements,

Whaling ships in Reykjavík harbour

and a visit is like a good punk anthem – it really packs a punch in a short amount of time! The owner is very friendly and informative.

The Harbour Area

Just north of the government district are the few streets that lead up to the harbour. These are full of cafés, bars and restaurants and are great for just wandering around. Hafnarstræti was once the old quayside and contains some of the city's oldest buildings; many of these have been beautifully restored. The Sæta Svínið Gastropub, Hafnarstræti 1–3, for example, was once the **Fálkahúsið**, where the king of Denmark kept his prize falcons. There are two carved wooden falcons on the roof to commemorate the fact. On Tryggvagata is **Hafnarhús** Ⓛ (Harbour House Art Museum; www.artmuseum.is; charge), one of three galleries belonging to the Reykjavík Art Museum, situated in the stylishly renovated former warehouse of the Port of Reykjavík. Here you will find on display a large collection by the internationally renowned Icelandic pop artist, Erró, as well as other contemporary artists from Iceland and elsewhere.

The modern **harbour** itself, built on reclaimed land, is still operational, with fishing boats bringing in their catch. In a good example of Icelandic contrariness, the **whale-watching boats** belonging to Elding (www.elding.is) and **Special Tours** (www.specialtours.is) share the dockside with **whaling ships**, recognisable from their black hulls and a red H on their funnels.

On the corner of the harbour is the **Sögusafnið** (Saga Museum; Grandagarður 2; www.sagamuseum.is; charge), a great place to take older children. This is Iceland's equivalent of Madame Tussaud's and an absorbing collection of life-size silicon models of the main characters from the sagas, which really brings the country's medieval history to life.

Next to the harbour is **Harpa Concert Hall** Ⓜ (www.harpa.is/en; free), which opened in 2011 and two years later won the European Union Prize for Contemporary Architecture, the Mies van der Rohe

WHERE TO SHOOT THE BEST PICTURES

Iceland is a photographer's playground, thanks to its endless expansive scenery, gothic-looking geology and of course the Northern Lights, visible anywhere between April and September.

The **Snæfellsnes Peninsula** offers a variety of alluring sights for photographers, including the **Djupalonssandur** black sand beach, hugged by an arc of lava cliffs. **Kirkjufell** mountain, with the Kirkjufellsfoss in the foreground, is another iconic scene. The black church of **Búðakirkja**, in the hamlet of Búðir, forms a dramatic subject against the windswept lava field.

The dreamy spa complex of the **Blue Lagoon** provides endless ways to get creative with images. The steaming water, backed by extinct volcanoes, forms an almost abstract setting.

Ethereal images galore are also available at the **Jökulsárlón** glacier lagoon, bordering Vatnajökull National Park. The still blue waters here are dotted with icebergs, which you can photograph from aboard a Zodiac boat on small-group tours.

Finally, **Seljalandsfoss**, two hours southeast of Reykjavíks, is one of the few waterfalls in Iceland that you can walk behind (during the summer months). This facilitates a panoramic shot, where the waterfall is lit by the golden rays of the midnight sun.

Award. Its glittering exterior, designed by artist Ólafur Elíasson to resemble the mosaic-like basalt columns found scattered throughout Iceland, reflects the sea and sky in a kaleidoscopic lightshow.

Along the bay to the east is Jón Gunnar Árnason's stunning sculpture *Sólfar (Sun Voyager*; 1986), which is based on a classic Viking longboat. Also worth a visit is the nearby **Living Art Museum** (Grandagarður 20; www.nylo.is; free), located in the historic Marshall House building.

Western Reykjavík

You will probably arrive in western Reykjavík where the bus terminals and domestic airport are situated, but there is little to tempt you out there again before your departure. The main exception is the excellent **Þjoðminjasafn Íslands** N (National Museum, Hringbraut, Suðurgata 1, junction with Hringbraut; www.thjodminjasafn.is; charge), which provides comprehensive insight into the past 1,200 years of Icelandic history. The section on the use of DNA testing is particularly interesting, detailing research work done on the teeth of the first settlers in order to determine their origins.

While in the vicinity, have a look too at **Norræna Húsið** O (Nordic House, Sturlugata 5; www.nordichouse.is; free except for some exhibitions), a Scandinavian cultural centre with a well-stocked library offering free internet access, exhibitions, concerts and a café.

Jón Gunnar Árnason's stainless steel Sólfar (Sun Voyager)

On the other side of the domestic airport, on **Öskjuhlíð** hill, is the glass-domed **Perlan** **P** (Pearl; https://perlan.is; charge), an exhibition centre and revolving restaurant that sits atop six enormous tanks used to store the geothermally heated water that supplies the city. The tanks hold 24 million litres (over 5 million gallons) of hot water and cater for almost half of Reykjavík's water consumption. Öskjuhlíð itself is a leafy area thanks to tree-planting schemes and the creation of walking and cycling paths.

At the southern edge of Öskjuhlíð is a seawater lagoon with its own mini-beach, **Nauthólsvík** **Q** (www.nautholsvik.is; charge), where the water is heated by the addition of hot water from the hill. The seawater here reaches 20°C (68°F), and there is a geothermal hot pot that gets even hotter (up to a bath-like 35°C/95°F).

Nauthólsvík beach

Eastern Reykjavík

There is more to see on the eastern side of the city. By the sea, isolated on a grassy square, is **Höfði House** **R**. The building is used for government receptions and social functions and hence closed to the public. Höfði was the location for the summit meetings in 1986 between presidents Reagan and Gorbachev to discuss global disarmament. A ghost supposedly haunts the house, but it was an electrical fault, rather than

SMOKY BAY'S STEAMY POWER

The name Reykjavík, meaning 'smoky bay', was coined by one of the early settlers who mistook the steam rising from the ground for smoke. Inevitably the arrival of man brought pollution in its wake, especially with the burning of fossil fuels. As the city massively expanded in the 20th century, so did the threat from polluted air. The decision, taken in the 1960s, to convert the city to environmentally friendly power sources cut carbon dioxide emissions from the heating system alone from 270,000 tonnes a year to virtually zero. Today, the geothermally heated water that gave the city its name is used to heat its buildings and is even piped beneath the pavements in winter to prevent icing. Reykjavík is arguably the world's greenest capital city.

the troublesome spectre, that was blamed for the fire that damaged the building in 2009.

Inland is **Kjarvalsstaðir** Ⓢ (Municipal Gallery, Flókagata; http://artmuseum.is/kjarvalsstadir; charge), another part of the Reykjavík Art Museum. Half the gallery is dedicated to the huge, colourful, often abstract landscapes by the Icelandic artist Jóhannes Kjarval (1885–1972), while the other half houses visiting exhibitions. Further east is **Ásmundarsafn** Ⓣ (Ásmundur Sveinsson Sculpture Museum, Sigtún 105; http://artmuseum.is/asmundarsafn; charge), a third part of the Reykjavík Art Museum. This is modern sculpture at its best, with huge figures depicting the people of Iceland as well as mythical characters.

A short distance to the east is the **Laugardalur** Ⓤ area, a green belt that serves as the capital's main sports area, with a large, open-air, geothermally heated swimming pool, soccer stadium, sports hall and ice-skating rink. There are also the Viking-themed mini-rides of the **Family Park** and the adjoining **Reykjavík Zoo** (www.mu.is; charge), which contains domestic farm animals, Arctic foxes, mink, reindeers, seals and a small cold water aquarium. The nearby

Botanical Gardens (www.grasagardur.is; free) has an impressive collection of 5,000 plants and almost all of Iceland's flora.

Viðey and Lundey

Just 1km (0.6 miles) out to sea due north of Reykjavík is the island of **Viðey** ⓥ, a haunting and historically significant place full of tussocked grass and soughing wind. Just up from the jetty is the oldest stone building in Iceland, Viðeyjarstofa, built in 1755 and now containing a summertime cafe. The bird life is prolific on Viðey, and there are some impressive basalt columns on the isthmus at the centre of the island, as well as some modern sculptures including Yoko Ono's Imagine Peace Tower, which lights up the sky on

The Ásmundarsafn sculpture museum

significant dates. Viðey is small enough to stroll around in an hour or two. Ferries depart from Sundahöfn harbour (Skarfabakki pier) in Reykjavík between mid-May and August at hourly intervals (for times, tel: 533 5055) and three times a day at the weekend in low season. The trip takes 5 minutes.

The best chance of seeing puffins close to the capital is on the tiny island of **Lundey**. Whale-watching tours (see page 41) sail past between mid-May and mid-August.

The Outskirts

Just outside Reykjavík there are a number of sights that can be visited on a short bus or taxi journey. To the east is **Árbæjarsafn** ⓦ (Arbær Open-Air Museum; https://reykjavikcitymuseum.is/arbaer-open-air-museum; charge). The original farm was mentioned in the sagas and is now a showcase for how Icelanders used to live. There are old homesteads with turf roofs, mostly relocated from the city centre, and a church that dates from 1842.

To the west is the town of **Hafnarfjörður** ❷, which was once a bigger port than Reykjavík, but is now considered more-or-less a suburb of the capital. The location is attractive, with parks and cliffs by the sea. **Fjörukráin** (Viking Village, Strandgata 50; www.fjorukrain.is) houses a guesthouse and the nation's only Viking restaurant. The best time to come here is in February when Viking-clad waiters serve traditional foods such as pickled rams' testicles and cured sharkmeat.

Hafnarborg Arts Centre (Strandgata 34; www.hafnarborg.is; free) is a genuine highlight of the town and has exhibitions by Icelandic and international artists, as well as occasional music recitals.

Hafnarfjörður Museum (https://byggdasafnid.is; free) is based across four separate sites: the two main buildings are **Pakkhúsið,** which contains an interesting canter through the town's history and a little toy museum; and **Sívertens-Hús**, the 19th-century home of local bigwig, Bjarni Sívertsen. There is a fine church and a **sculpture garden** at Viðistaðir on the northern outskirts of the town.

NOTES

Reykjavík is increasingly popular as a destination for cruise ships. Over 320,000 visitors a year come to Iceland this way. The vessels moor in the main harbour.

The Blue Lagoon

One trip out of Reykjavík that should not be missed is to the world's greatest outdoor bath, **Bláa Loníð** ❸ (Blue Lagoon, Grindavík; www.bluelagoon.com; charge). Most hotels will have details of tours, but you can also arrive by public bus. The lagoon is a pool of seawater naturally heated by the geothermal activity below the surface. It sits in the middle of a lava field and you can lounge around here with warm mud oozing between your toes in wonderfully warm water temperatures of 37–40°C (98–104°F) all year round.

In spite of its name, the lagoon is not a natural phenomenon, but a fortuitous by-product of Iceland's geo-thermal energy usage. The nearby Svartsengi power plant pumps mineral-laden water from up to 2km (1.2 miles) beneath the earth's surface, at a temperature of 240°C (470°F). The superheated water passes through a dual process, on the one hand to generate electricity, and on the other to heat fresh water. This run-off water, rich in silica, salt and other elements, once flowed out into a pool a few hundred metres from the present lagoon's site. Psoriasis and eczema sufferers noticed that bathing in the water seemed to ease their symptoms. Once the word was out, the lagoon was moved to its current location, and state-of-the-art facilities, carefully designed to complement the surrounding landscape, were built around it.

A cave-like sauna is carved into the lava and a thundering waterfall delivers a pounding massage. The complex also contains a spa treatment area, restaurant, snack bar, shop, conference facilities, and, should you care to spend the night, there is a guesthouse just over the lava field. All summer long (June–Aug), however, the changing rooms get crowded and it may be worth getting up early to beat the crowds. If you are impressed by the Blue Lagoon's healing properties, a range of eponymous skin and bathing products are on sale across the island.

The Golden Circle

Highlights

- **Þingvellir**, see page 50
- **Skálholt**, see page 52
- **Geysir**, see page 52
- **Gullfoss**, see page 53

This 300km (190-mile) round trip from Reykjavík takes in some of the key historical and geological sites in Iceland. They include the original geyser that gave its name to gushing blowholes worldwide, the site of the country's first parliament, and one of its most dramatic waterfalls. You can cover the route on any one of a number of day tours from Reykjavík. They take about seven hours, but include stops at gift shops and eating places along the way. The trip can just about be done by public transport or you could hire a car. The route is well signposted, and parking is good.

The Blue Lagoon

Þingvellir

The nearest landmark to the capital on the Golden Circle route is the site of the original Alþingi (parliament), established in 930. It is situated in **Þingvellir** ❹, pronounced Thingvellir, a national park that has enormous political and geographical significance. Unfortunately, there are few actual monuments or buildings to be seen, and you have to use your imagination to picture the events of the past.

There is a well-marked **information centre** (www.thingvellir.is) with a cafe and a shop selling maps and books about the area. Fishing and camping permits can be obtained here. It's worth familiarising yourself with the layout of the park before you set off to explore as it's not that well signposted.

Þingvellir, a national park and site of the original parliament

THE PARLIAMENT AT ÞINGVELLIR

Þingvellir may feel as if it's in the middle of nowhere, but 1,000 years ago it was the focal point of the country. For two weeks every summer Icelanders flooded into the valley to take part in or just watch the proceedings of the Alþingi (parliament). The position was perfect, with plenty of grazing land for horses, good tracks from the more populated parts of Iceland and a lake teeming with fish to feed the multitudes. Trading and socialising went on continuously while the leaders got on with the serious work of running the country. It was the job of the 36 chieftains from the various regions to agree on new laws, under the supervision of the 'lawspeaker'. A Law Council, made up of four regional courts and a supreme court, dealt with infringements and disputes – outlawry was the most severe sentence that could be passed. However, once the Alþingi's judgment had been made, the system relied on the wronged party enforcing the punishment. Parliament itself had no power to stop feuds or even open warfare from breaking out when grievances could not be settled. From the mid-16th century the courts gained more power, and Þingvellir became a site of public punishment and execution, reflected in many of its grisly placenames. Men were beheaded, adulterous women drowned, and unfortunate souls convicted of witchcraft were burned alive. Alþingi's last meeting was held here in 1798; after that a national court and parliament was established in Reykjavík.

The park is situated on top of the line where the North American and Eurasian continental plates meet. In fact they are slowly drifting apart at a rate of 2cm (0.78in) a year. Above the rift, at the **Almannagjá viewing point**, there is the interpretive **centre** containing interactive displays about the national park. From up here, you can clearly see the rift valley as you look towards the lake. The red-roofed church dates from 1859. It stands on the site of a much bigger church that held sway over all the local inhabitants. Below you is the Alþingi site itself. You can walk down into it; a flagpole marks where the leader of the parliament, the law speaker, made his proclamations. Just to the east of the Alþingi, the Öxará River flows into a lake, **Þingvallavatn**. There's a 20 metre (66ft) waterfall, and nearby you can clearly see the layers of ash left by successive eruptions.

Skálholt

Next stop on the Golden Circle is **Skálholt** ❺, about 45km (28 miles) to the east of Þingvellir. It is hard to imagine that this was once the biggest settlement in Iceland, as there is little to see here today; but for over 700 years, from 1056 onwards, this was a seat of enormous ecclesiastical power. A massive earthquake destroyed Skálholt's cathedral in the late 18th century, when the bishop picked up his cassock and headed for the relative safety of Reykjavík. The present church was built in 1963. Inside you can see the coffin of one of the early bishops, uncovered during the building work, and a fine modern mosaic above the altar. Iceland's oldest music festival, of early and contemporary classical music, is held here in July (www.sumartonleikar.is).

Skálholt, once the biggest settlement in Iceland

Geysir

Another 20km (12 miles) to the northeast you can see evidence of the one power that both church and state have to respect – nature. There are bigger geysers (*geysir* in Icelandic) in the world, and more impressive ones, but this is the original. **Geysir** ❻ is one of the few Icelandic words to have made it into the lexicon of world language. Sadly, the gusher that used to reach heights of 60m (200ft) hasn't performed well for decades. For years, Icelanders poured masses of soap powder into the orifice to make it perform, but in the end they gave up. It still erupts on odd occasions, but generally only to a height of around 10 metres (33ft)

Gullfoss carving out a canyon

Fortunately, there is the smaller, but far more reliable **Strokkur** (literally 'the churn') beside Geysir: Strokkur spurts to a height of around 20m (66ft) every few minutes, without artificial encouragement.

The whole Geysir area is geothermically active and smells strongly of sulphur (similar to the smell rotten eggs). Walking trails are marked out among the steaming vents and glistening, multi-coloured mud formations. Don't be tempted to poke your fingers into any pools: an average of seven tourists are badly burned every week during the summer months.

Gullfoss

An example of nature at its most forceful is to be found another 6km (4 miles) along the road to the north. **Gullfoss** ❼ (Golden

Falls; http://gullfoss.is) is, in fact, two separate waterfalls a short distance apart. Their combined drop is 32 metres (105ft), and the pounding water then thunders away along the 2km (1.2-mile) -long canyon below. Several paths lead above and alongside the waterfall, allowing you to get within an arm's length of the awesome flow. Wear a raincoat, or the clouds of spray that create dozens of photogenic rainbows on sunny days will douse you from head to foot.

The falls were nearly destroyed by a hydroelectric dam project in the 1920s but the plans were halted. The government instead purchased the falls and made them a national monument.

The West Coast

Highlights

- **Akranes**, see below
- **Borgarnes**, see page 55
- **Reykholt and Vicinity**, see page 55
- **The Snæfellsnes Peninsula**, see page 57

The wild Snæfellsnes peninsula is within day-trip striking-distance of Reykjavík, and as such is a growing tourist destination. Most tour companies offer a circuit of its rocky coves, extinct glacier-topped volcano **Snæfellsjökull**, and traditional fishing villages such as Ólafsvík and Stykkishólmur. On the way, several settlements hold cultural surprises.

Akranes

Located just north of Reykjavík, **Akranes** ❽ is dominated by fish-processing, trawler production and cement making. Far more appealing is the **Byggðasafninu í Görðum** (Akranes Folk Museum; www.museum.is; charge), east of town. It houses a folk museum with the emphasis on maritime history, including a well-preserved *ketch*, one of the first decked fishing boats in Iceland. The museum also has the country's largest collection of rocks, minerals and fossils. There are swimming pools and four hotpots adjacent on Garðar.

Stykkishólmur harbour

Borgarnes

Borgarnes ❾ on the windswept west coast, is essentially a service centre for the neighbouring dairy farms. The park, known as **Skallagrímsgarður**, commemorates one of Iceland's first settlers, Skallagrímur Kveldúlfsson, whose burial mound is still visible. His son, Egill, was the hero of *Egils Saga,* and there is a monument to him by the mound. **The Settlement Centre of Iceland** (www.landnam.is; charge), in a restored warehouse by the harbour, offers up two striking exhibitions. One explores the settlement of Iceland, and the other uses striking sound and visuals to tell the tale of Egill and his bloodthirsty deeds.

Reykholt and Vicinity

Both its setting and its cultural history make **Reykholt** ❿ a place worth visiting. The wide, open spaces of its valley setting are refreshing after so many mountains and were once home to Snorri Sturluson, born in 1179 and immortalised by his saga-writing. He was a distinguished scholar but was murdered here in 1241 after falling foul of the Norwegian king. You can visit **Snorralaug**, the bathing pool

Snorralaug bathing pool

where the chieftain would receive visitors and, beside it, the partly restored remains of a tunnel that led to his farmhouse. **Snorrastofa** (www.snorrastofa.is; charge), located just next to the church, is a research centre dedicated to Snorri, and contains an exhibition about his life and work.

At **Húsafell**, to the east, many Icelanders have holiday cottages from which they explore the surrounding area. Nearby is the magnificent **Hraunfossar**, a multitude of tiny cascades that tumble into the Hvíta River along a 1km (0.6-mile) stretch. Further afield is a forest and two **glaciers**, Þórisjökull and Eiríksjökull, as well as several **lava caves** hidden inside the 52km-long Hallmundarhraun lava flow, including Víðgelmir at the farm Fljótstunga (www.thecave.is). Húsafell is also the starting point for the excursions into the heart of Iceland's second largest glacier – **Langjökull**. Into the Glacier operates tours to this unique, man-made labyrinth of 500m (1,584-ft) -long, artificially lit corridors and caves that have been dug into the glacier's cap. See https://intotheglacier.is for more details.

Further north is the reconstructed farmhouse of **Eiríksstaðir** (www.eiriksstadir.is; charge), from which the Vikings launched their westward voyages of discovery. Eirík the Red, after whom the farm is named, went on to discover Greenland, while his son, Leifur, was the first European to set foot in America. There is a reconstruction of the original farm, complete with Viking guides, next to the excavated hall; the latter dates from 890–980.

The Snæfellsnes Peninsula

At 1,445 metres (4,740ft) high, **Snæfellsjökull** ⓫ is permanently snow-capped. It was made famous worldwide by Jules Verne as the entry point for his *Journey to the Centre of the Earth* and also plays a role in *Under the Glacier*, by Nobel Prize-winning Icelandic novelist Halldór Laxness. The glacier is popular for snowmobile tours. The main peak itself is a less daunting climb than it looks, but it's best to go with gear (crampons) and a guide, due to crevasses on the glacier.

A breathtaking view from Snæfellsjökull

From late May to August, Láki Tours run whale-watching trips (www.lakitours.com) from **Ólafsvík**, where there's a good chance of spotting minke, white-beaked dolphin and other cetaceans. In winter (November to April), killer whales follow the herring into Grundarfjörður, and Láki sail out from the village of the same name to greet them.

Further along the north coast, **Stykkishólmur** ⓬ is an attractive place with brightly painted wooden houses down by the harbour. At the quayside, it's possible to take a two-hour birdwatching and scallop-tasting tour. There is an unusual modern **church** overlooking the town, its interior lit by hundreds of bulbs that seem to drip from the ceiling. Classical music concerts take place here in summer. The town's former library has an equally watery feel; the American artist Roni Horn converted into an art installation Vatnasafn (www.libraryofwater.is; charge). South of the town is the mountain of **Helgafell**, much talked about in Icelandic folklore, but not much more than a hillock. It is said that you can have three wishes granted if you climb it in silence from the west and then descend to the east without looking back.

Flatey island

A car/passenger ferry sails from Stykkishólmur to the West Fjords, calling in at the delightful island of **Flatey** ⓭ in summer. It is a sleepy, peaceful little place, with restored wooden houses set among bright yellow fields of buttercups. The eastern part of the island is a **nature reserve** teeming with birdlife. Watch out for the Arctic terns, which seem particularly aggressive here – even the island's sheep aren't immune from their dive-bombing attacks. There is a fine little church, which was painted by the Catalan artist Baltasar in return for free accommodation, and, next door, the oldest and smallest library in Iceland. Overnight accommodation is available in summer.

The West Fjords

Highlights

- **Ísafjörður**, see below
- **Hornstrandir Peninsula**, see page 60

Travellers in the West Fjords face some of the worst roads in the country and the often-inhospitable climate means it is a relatively little-visited part of Iceland. Yet the region offers Iceland's most dramatic, craggy fjords and some of its best hiking, while soaring cliffs host literally millions of breeding sea birds.

Ísafjörður and Around

The only town of any real size in the region is **Ísafjörður** ⓮. The deep harbour helped it to become an important fishing community, and now plays host to cruise ships too. For a taste of how tough life in these parts once was, visit the **West Fjords Heritage Museum** (Sudurtangi; www.nedsti.is; charge). Housed in a restored timber warehouse, exhibits trace the development of the town and its fishing industry, with all sorts of nautical paraphernalia. The town has a swimming pool, cinema and a few restaurants.

About 12km (7 miles) north, **Bolungarvík** is an exposed spot, liable to landslides and avalanches. It has a couple of

Ísafjörður in the Westfjords

little museums. The **Ósvör Maritime Museum** (www.bolungarvik.is/osvor; charge) is in a restored fishing station and the **Natural History Museum** (Aðalstræti 21; www.bolungarvik.is/nabo; charge) has a jumble of stuffed animals including a seal and polar bear. Further west, the coast is largely uninhabited; the scenery is wild and imposing, a mixture of wind-lashed headlands and mighty snow-capped peaks.

Southeast of Ísafjörður, the road winds around several fjords to the village of **Reykjanes**, which is worth a stop for its heated outdoor pool and sauna. If you want to get close to a glacier, continue towards the **Kaldalón glacial lagoon**. From the head of the lagoon you can follow a walking trail for about an hour and a half to the tip of the glacier.

The area further north towards the **Hornstrandir Peninsula** ⓯ is now uninhabited, after the last family left it in 1995. The beauty of this part of the country is astonishing with its sandy bays, rugged cliffs, meadows of wildflowers and massive bird colonies. For serious hiking it's hard to beat, and you can literally walk all day without meeting anyone. If you're lucky you might spot an Arctic fox and, offshore, whales and seals.

West of Ísafjörður, the road runs through some tiny fishing villages as it heads south. There is a breath-taking descent into

Hrafnseyri, the birthplace of the Independence leader, Jón Sigurðsson. A small museum is dedicated to his memory (www.hrafnseyri.is; charge), and there is much celebration in the village on Independence Day, 17 June. The **Dynjandi waterfall**, meaning 'the thundering one', just south of here, is a spectacular collection of cascades.

To the west, **Tálknafjörður** is a lively spot. It has a good swimming pool, bike hire, an adventure centre offering watersports and walking, and even a bar. Up the hillside are two open-air geothermal hotpots, Pollurinn, with beautiful views of the fjord.

Látrabjarg is the most westerly point in Europe. What makes the long, pothole-filled journey worthwhile is the sense of bleakness and the plunging **bird cliffs**. Thousands of puffins nest here in burrows, and you can get surprisingly close to them. There are at least as many guillemots, too, plus the largest colony of razorbills in the world. In spite of the numbers, birdwatching is not as easy here as elsewhere in the country, because the cliffs form such a long, straight line.

Dynjandi falls

There is a wonderful **beach** at nearby **Rauðasandur**, with pink sand and superb surf thundering in from the Atlantic. **Hnjótur** is home to the **Egill Ólafsson Museum** (www.hnjotur.is; charge),

The coastline of Surtsey Island, one of the Westman Islands

one man's odd-ball collection of marine rescue equipment, old telephones and a typewriter with Icelandic characters. The prize exhibit is a rusting Aeroflot biplane that ended up in Iceland after its pilot, fleeing Russia, was refused permission to land in the US. Outside is a replica Viking longship, a gift from Norway to mark 1,100 years of settlement.

The Westman Islands

Highlights

- **Heimaey**, see page 63

The **Westman Islands** ⓰, or *Vestmannaeyjar* to give them their Icelandic name, are a long strip of 16 islands and numerous rocks or skerries about 10km (6 miles) off the south coast of Iceland. Carbon dating has suggested that they may have been the first part of the country to be inhabited. They were created by underwater eruptions, and the process is still ongoing: the newest island, Surtsey, emerged from the sea in the mid-1960s. It has been studied with fascination by scientists, not just because of its dramatic appearance, but for the flora and fauna that are taking root and making it their home.

The tourist authorities describe the islands as the 'Capri of the North', although even they wouldn't claim it was anything to do with the weather. The coves and inlets may be reminiscent of the chic Italian island, but the rain and wind that batter them for much of the year certainly are not.

Heimaey

The only inhabited island is **Heimaey**, which can be reached by ferry (see page 141) or plane, although low cloud can close the airport at short notice. The island has a pretty and petite town, but most visitors come for the surrounding countryside and especially the **bird cliffs**. Millions of puffins used to come here every year to nest and breed on the precipitous cliffs, although numbers are declining rapidly. You can reach them on foot or take

Heimaey Island

a boat out and get a view from the sea. You might also see whales and seals in the waters around the islands.

The other big draw of Heimaey is the landscape. Two dramatic cones rise up just outside the town: the volcano, Helgafell, and a much newer mountain, Eldfell, created in a massive eruption in 1973 that almost buried the town. In the early hours of 23 January 1973, a fissure nearly 2km (1-mile) long opened up on the eastern side of Helgafell. Red-hot lava started to spurt into the sky, heralding an eruption that was to last for the next six months. The threat to the town was immediate and the entire 5,000-strong population was evacuated to the mainland. Flying bombs of molten lava crashed through windows or melted through roofs, and a colossal river of lava made its way towards the town. Many houses collapsed under the weight of falling ash and by the time the flow stopped, a third of Heimaey had been destroyed. When it was all over, the island was 2.2 sq km (0.84 sq miles) larger, and the new mountain of Eldfell had been created.

THE PUFFIN POPULATION

The colourful Atlantic puffin – with its large, stripy beak and bright orange legs and feet – is a great favourite with visitors. Puffins are highly sociable, often standing about in groups and nesting in large colonies. They fish together, too, forming wide rafts out to sea. They can dive to 60 metres (200ft) in search of fish, but also eat plankton in winter. They rarely travel far from their colony while raising their young. Both parents incubate a single egg. The males and females look very similar, but neither grow much more than 30cm (12in) in height. The birds are hunted for food in Iceland, fished out of the air with huge nets. They produce a dark meat, like duck but less fatty, often served with a blueberry sauce. However, concerns over declining puffin colonies have led to a hunting ban in the Westman Islands, once the capital of puffin-hunting.

Millions of Atlantic puffins breed in Iceland

At the edge of the lava, the rather curious Pompeii of the North project has excavated some of the ruined houses on the former street of Suðurvegur. You can learn more about this and other eruptions at the **Eldheimar Museum** (http://eldheimar.is; charge), where audio guides are offered in English.

A walking path runs round the whole island, along some of the best bird cliffs, out to Storhöfði (the island's southernmost tip and the windiest place in Iceland), and back over the new lava to the pretty Skansinn area. Paths also lead to the top of the steep harbourside cliffs – these require careful climbing.

The Westman Islanders are great sports enthusiasts. There are four football fields on the islands and a modern sports centre with a pool. You can easily take in some fishing, horse riding or golf if you stay for long enough.

The South Coast

Highlights

- **Þórsmörk**, see below
- **Skógar**, see page 67
- **Vík**, see page 68
- **Vatnajökull**, see page 69
- **Jökulsárlón**, see page 71
- **Höfn**, see page 71

The stretch of highway that runs east along the south of Iceland is a mixture of long, almost featureless lava fields and wonderful views of the mountain and glaciers that come down to the sea in the southeast. It has a reputation as the wettest part of the country, but if the weather holds it is also one of the most dramatic.

As you leave Reykjavík and pass **Selfoss**, heading east, look out for **Mt Hekla**. On a fine day its cone provides a perfect backdrop to Reykjavík, but it's frequently shrouded in cloud. It is an active volcano that has wiped out farming in the surrounding area several times and erupted every 10 years or so since 1970; however, it can still be climbed fairly easily. Off the ringroad, on Rte 26, the historical (and reputedly haunted) farm of Leirubakki has a small exhibition (www.leirubakki.is; charge) about the volcano.

Þórsmörk

You are now entering saga country and, in particular, the setting for the bloodiest of the sagas – that which tells the story of the wise and decent Njál and the gruesome end that met most of his friends and family. Much of the action took place at the Alþingi at Þingvellir (see page 50), but there was more than a little blood-letting near the village of Hvolsvöllur, where there is now an Icelandic Saga Centre with background information on the various tales. Here, there is a turning northeast to **Þórsmörk** ⓱, a beautiful nature reserve sheltered between three glaciers. City dwellers from Reykjavík flock here in summer to enjoy mountain walks and lovely views. Note that you have to ford several glacial rivers to get to Þórsmörk, so the route is only open to 4WDs or mountain buses, not ordinary cars.

Skógar

This area sits under Eyjafjallajökull: the 2010 eruptions under the glacier covered everything for miles around in thick grey ash. 10km (6.2 miles) east, tiny **Skógar** ⓲ is home to a meticulously managed folk museum (www.skogasafn.is; charge). It contains a 6,000-piece collection and has some fascinating historical buildings in the grounds, including a reconstructed church, a school and a driftwood house.

Beautiful scenery around Þórsmörk

Skógar homestead

There is a splendid waterfall, Skógafoss, the sheer fall of which offers one of south Iceland's best photo opportunities. The trek from here to Þórsmörk, passing between the ice-caps of Eyjafjallajökull and Myrdalsjökull over the Fimmvörðuháls pass, is popular with the hardy and becomes quite crowded, particularly in July. There are two huts between the ice-caps: one is an emergency shelter, the other is pre-bookable.

Vík

Continuing east, the distinctive rock arch at **Dyrhólaey** is a nature reserve packed full of nesting seabirds. The next major stop is the coastal town of **Vík** ⓳, or to give its full name, Vík í Mýrdal (Bay of the Marshy Valley). It's a pretty little town, with a beach of black volcanic sand, jagged cliffs and lots of birdlife. Three steeples of stone, known as **Reynisdrangar** (Troll Rocks), rise out of the sea. Legend has it that they are the figures of trolls that turned to stone when they failed to get under cover before the sun hit them. Far more monstrous are the aggressive Arctic terns – Vík contains one of Iceland's largest breeding colonies!

The road crosses more barren fields of lava and *sandur*, a mix of silt, sand and gravel. Oddly shaped boulders are partly overgrown with lichens, helping to give the area a somewhat otherworldly feel. Little wooden bridges cross the rivers, reducing the highway to one lane. In the middle of all this is the tiny hamlet of **Kirkjubæjarklaustur**, a good place to pick up provisions. While doing so, you can reflect on the power of prayer, for it was here that the local pastor delivered his 'Fire Sermon', which believers will tell you halted the flow of lava during the Lakagígar eruption of 1783 and saved the church. A memorial chapel, built in 1974, commemorates the miracle.

A rough road, which is accessible only to 4WD vehicles, goes from Kirkjubæjarklaustur to the **Lakagígar Crater Row**, where you can see some of the effects of the 1783 eruptions, which lasted for 10 months and were known as the Skaftáreldar (Skaftá river fires). This was one of the largest effusive eruptions ever recorded, producing about 12 cubic km (2.87 cubic miles). Most of Iceland's livestock died from the poisonous fumes. Some 100 craters extend for 25km (15 miles) up to the glacier; the surrounding lava field is dotted with caves and other lava formations. It takes several hours to see them properly, but there are amazing views from the top of Mt Laki– a climb of about an hour.

Rock formations near Kirkjubæjarklaustur

Vatnajökull

The massive **Vatnajökull** ⓴, the biggest ice-cap in Europe, is almost 150km (90 miles) across and dominates the southeastern corner of Iceland. Driving around the ring road you can get fascinating glimpses of it as it breaks through the mountains. To get close to the ice-cap, you have to leave the main road and head inland, thought its size and beauty is best appreciated from the air: internal scheduled flights from Reykjavík to Egilsstaðir or Höfn pass close by, or you can take a sightseeing flight from the small airfield at Skaftafell.

In October 1996, the world's media besieged Vatnajökull when a fissure 4km (2.48-miles) long opened beneath the surface of the glacier. Within two days a 10km (6-mile) column of steam was rising above the ice.

Massive flooding was predicted, but the eruption fizzled out, and the journalists departed. Then, on 5 November, the ice dam broke and a huge surge of water burst forth, destroying bridges and roads and carrying massive ice blocks with it.

Svartifoss, the Black Falls

A number of smaller valley glaciers, all linked to Vatnajökull, are most clearly visible from the road. One of these, Skaftafellsjökull, stops close to **Skaftafell** ㉑ (visitor centre; for details check www.vatnajokulsthjodgardur.is), part of Vatnajökull National Park. In the shadow of Iceland's highest peak, **Hvannadalshnúkur** (2,120m/6,950ft), this is serious walking territory and very popular in summer. But with so many trails into the hills, it's not difficult to find solitude.

Hikers take daylong round trips to the higher moorlands and peaks, such as those at **Kristínartindur**. Among the shorter walks is the route up to **Svartifoss** (Black Falls), named after the surrounding sombre cliffs of basalt, and the wheelchair-accessible path to the edge of the Skaftafellsjökull glacier tongue.

Jökulsárlón

Continuing east, the next major point of interest is the extraordinary glacier river lagoon at **Jökulsárlón** ㉒. This photogenic spot is just off the road where a small bridge crosses the mouth of the lake. Great slabs of ice that have broken off the **Breiðamerkurjökull** valley glacier float eerily in the water, some as big as houses. There are around 40 boat cruises daily in summer around Jökulsárlón, weaving among the glistening ice formations.

Höfn

The final outpost in southeastern Iceland is the town of **Höfn** ㉓, which translates simply as 'harbour'. If you are heading for the Eastfjords (see page 93) by public transport, you might find yourself staying overnight here. It's not the most exciting of places, but it's the largest settlement for miles around. Höfn is famous for its langoustines, and is liveliest during the annual Lobster Festival (Humarhátíð; www.hornafjordur.is), held at the end of June. South of the harbour is Ósland, a promontory with rich birdlife (particularly Arctic tern), from where there are fabulous

The glacier lagoon at Jökulsárlón

mountain-and-glacier views. Tours of the icecap by 4WD can be organised from Höfn.

The North Coast

Highlights

- **Akureyri**, see page 73
- **Eyjafjörður**, see page 76
- **West of Akureyri**, see page 78
- **Húsavík**, see page 81

If you are restricted to just one part of the country in addition to Reykjavík, there is a good chance you will choose the north coast. It's the most accessible region to reach and, in many ways, the liveliest. Akureyri is generally considered to be the capital of the north, and Húsavík is reputedly the best place in Iceland for whale-watching. Despite being close to the Arctic Circle, the north also has the best weather, and temperatures can reach 20°C (68°F) or more in summer. The coastline is very dramatic in places, and there are some huge fjords – a feature that is almost completely lacking in the south.

Akureyri

Whether you fly, drive or take a bus you are almost certain to end up in **Akureyri** ㉔. It is an attractive place and has a lot more life about it than most provincial towns. It is home to the only professional theatre in Iceland outside the capital, as well as the only university. Many parts of the country suffer from an exodus of young people, but not Akureyri, which has a youthful feel about it. In summer the town is busy with tourists; in winter it's a major destination for conferences.

Akureyri is surrounded by high mountains, which are up to 1,500 metres (5,000ft) tall and snowcapped for much of the year. Green and lush in comparison to many other towns, it even has its own forest, botanical garden and a golf course (every June the Arctic Open tees

Akureyrarkirkja

off under the midnight sun). Akureyri is also a good starting point for visiting some of the most beautiful parts of the country, both to the east and the west.

The centre of town is compact. The main shopping street is the pedestrianised **Hafnarstræti**, where the hustle and bustle (such as it is) of this small town's life takes place. An Akureyri institution, the Bautinn restaurant (www.bautinn.is) at no.92, sits on a crossroads and is a good place to watch the world go by. Hafnarstræti runs from close to the huge main church towards the rather nondescript town square, Ráðhústorg. Running east from the square is Strandgata, which has become the trendy corner of town; this leads down to the port, where cruise liners dock in summer.

The twin spires of the **Akureyrarkirkja** (www.akureyrarkirkja.is; free) tower over the town, most dramatically at night when they are spotlit against the dark sky. Fusing Art Deco and traditional Nordic styles, the church was designed by architect Guðjón Samúelsson, who was also responsible for the vast Hallsgrímskirkja in Reykjavík (see page 35). Inside is a fine stained-glass window, imported from the original cathedral at Coventry in the English Midlands. The window was removed at the start of World War II, before the cathedral was destroyed by bombs; it was rescued from a London antiques shop and now forms the centrepiece of an impressive display that also features scenes from Iceland's own history.

Having clambered up to the church, there is a gentler climb to another of the town's main attractions, the **Lystigarðurinn** (Botanical Garden; Eyrarlandsvegur; www.lystigardur.akureyri.is; free). The gardens are famed for their 7,000 species of local and foreign flowers, from southern Europe, Africa, South America and Australasia, all blooming merrily in Akureyri's warm microclimate. The gardens were set up by a local women's association in 1912 to provide a relaxing atmosphere for families. They are very well kept, and are the perfect place to relax on a sunny day: the lovely cafe by the top entrance is open year-round.

Akureyri was the birthplace of the Jesuit priest, Jón Sveinsson, whose children's books were translated into 40 languages. At Aðalstræti 54, you can visit **Nonnahús** (www.minjasafnid.is; charge), the tiny black wooden house where he lived with his widowed mother and five siblings.

Nearby, **Minjasafnið á Akureyri** (Akureyri Municipal Museum; Aðalstræti 58; www.minjasafnid.is; charge) has a wide collection of everyday items that date as far back as the settlement in the 9th century, including a beautifully painted pulpit. The church here is still used for weddings. **Listasafnið á Akureyri** (Kaupvangsstræti

Akureyri Botanical Garden

12; www.listak.is; charge) is the town's **Art Museum** and offers visitors one of the best insights into the town's present-day cultural life.

The town's **swimming pool** (Þingvallastræti 21; tel: 461 4455; charge) is one of the best in the country, with two outdoor pools, an indoor pool, two waterslides, hot tubs, a steam room and sauna. In summer, there are extra distractions for children, including minigolf and electric cars.

An hour's walk south of the town is one of Iceland's few wooded areas at **Kjarnaskógur**. Given the shortage of trees in Iceland, this is considered something of an attraction, and the townspeople flock here on sunny weekends. There is a children's play area, picnic sites and a jogging track.

Eyjafjörður

From Akureyri two roads fork off to the north along each side of Eyjafjörður fjord. The cluster of towns and villages on the banks of the fjord are hemmed in close to the water by high mountains. The land here is particularly fertile, and the mild climate makes it good farming territory. It is a suitable area for exploring both on land and at sea, with ferry links to the islands of Grímsey and Hrísey.

Dalvík, a fishing village about an hour's drive north of Akureyri, was rebuilt after an earthquake in 1934 demolished half its buildings, but the harbour front is still attractive. The town has a good outdoor swimming pool and an interesting museum, **Byggðasafnið Hvoll** (www.dalvikurbyggd.is/hvoll; charge), which contains photographs of Iceland's

NOTES

Iceland's tallest man, Jóhann Kristinn Pétursson, known as Jóhann the Giant, was an impressive 2.34 metres (7ft 8in) tall. Born in 1913, he worked in circuses and shows across Europe and the United States. He returned to Dalvík late in his life and died there in 1984.

White-tailed ptarmigan, Vatnajökull glacier

tallest man, Jóhann Kristinn Pétursson (see box) and many of his possessions.

The main reason that people come to Dalvík is to catch the ferry to the island of **Grímsey** ㉕. The Arctic Circle runs through the centre of this island: once you've crossed it, you can buy yourself a commemorative certificate from the local cafe. The small settlement of **Sandvík** has some basic services, including a swimming pool. The community centre commemorates the island's benefactor, Daniel Willard Fiske, a 19th-century American chess champion who had read about its reputation for producing great chess players since Viking days. He left money for a school and library to be built and donated 11 marble chessboards. The locals still celebrate his birthday on 11 November although hardly any of them play chess anymore.

Grímsey is well known for its extensive **birdlife** – the craggy cliffs on the north and east of the island are home to about 60 species, including puffins, kittiwakes and razorbills. You can explore on your own or find a local guide in the town. The only proper road runs along the west side of Grímsey from Sandvík to the airport, from where there are regular flights to Akureyri. The runway has to be regularly cleared of birds, and this is sometimes done by incoming flights buzzing the airstrip before coming round again to land.

The Dalvík–Grímsey ferry stops at the island of **Hrísey**; there is also a far more frequent service from Árskógssandur, just south of Dalvík, departing every two hours in summer. Iceland's second-largest island is another choice destination for bird lovers. It is particularly famous for its fearless ptarmigan; they are prolific all year round, although their number swells in the autumn, and they can often be seen waddling down the streets. There are around 40 species of birds on the island, and it is an important breeding ground for eider ducks and Arctic tern.

On the eastern side of the fjord the first place of interest is the fishing village of **Svalbarðseyri**. According to local folklore, this is home to a large community of elves who live in the cliffs behind the village. Even if this sounds all rather unlikely, you are still sure to be enchanted here by the rugged coastline.

At **Laufás**, around 30km (19 miles) north of Akureyri, there is a magnificent example of a 19th-century turf farmhouse, maintained by Akureyri Museum (www.minjasafnid.is; charge). Inside there is a multitude of effects showing how life was lived here more than 100 years ago. The timber church dates from 1865.

West of Akureyri

On the route west, the tiny village of **Hofsós** is home to **Vesturfarasetrið** (Icelandic Emigration Centre; http://hofsos.is; charge). If you think you are of Icelandic descent, this is the place to come to try to trace your roots. It is not just for genealogists, though – there is a great exhibition telling the story of those Icelanders who emigrated west to the New World. A small but astonishing outdoor **swimming pool** (www.facebook.com/sundlauginhofsosi; charge) in Hofsós overlooks the fjord: it's not uncommon to see whales swim past as you're doing your lengths.

Hólar í Hjaltadal, 25km (15 miles) southeast and inland from the coast road, was once a thriving cultural and religious centre. Until the Reformation, it was a great seat of learning, with monks studying the scriptures and transcribing manuscripts. It housed the country's first printing press, dating from 1530. A red-stone **cathedral** (mid-May–Aug daily 10am–6pm), dating from 1759–63, commemorates its religious past. There is sacred art and sculpture

Laufás turf farmhouse

on display, as well as a modern mosaic by the artist Erró. The bones of the last Catholic bishop in Iceland, Jón Arason, are buried here. He was beheaded in 1550 for resisting the spread of the protestant Reformation. In summer, classical concerts are held here.

Another important historical site is **Þingeyrar**, 85km (53 miles) further west. It was the home of one of the first regional assemblies, as well as the first monastery in 1133. It was here that many of the sagas were first written, and other texts were transcribed by the monks. The monastery disappeared after the Reformation, but there is an impressive 19th-century church, **Þingeyrarkirkja** (www.thingeyri.is/thingeyri/thingeyrarkirkja; free), made of basalt, that is visible for miles around. The interior has white walls, green

Hólar cathedral, with its detached bell tower

WHALES AND WHALING

For many visitors, Iceland's attitude to whaling is perplexing. The country has an excellent record for environmental protection and an apparent deep respect for nature. Nevertheless, whaling is a topic that continues to arouse passionate nationalistic feelings in Iceland, with polls indicating widespread popular support for the commercial hunt.

The abundance of whales off Iceland's coasts inevitably led to them being caught and killed for food. In 1948 this developed into a commercial whaling industry that continued until 1989, when strong international pressure led to a break in whaling.

In 2020, Covid-19 pandemic restrictions combined with a decreasing market for whale meat in Japan saw Iceland pause its whaling activities; but any hopes that this would be a permanent measure were soon dashed, and in 2024 the government issued whaling licenses for the next five years.

Still, Icelandic whaling is a strange kettle of fish. Only around five percent of Icelanders eat whale regularly: tourists are now its main devourers within the domestic market. The rest, including meat from endangered fin whales, is exported to Japan, for human consumption and for luxury dog treats. The Icelandic government has insisted that whale-hunting quotas are "well within the generally accepted values for sustainable catch rates of whale stocks". Opposition to the whaling industry as a whole historically mainly came from outside, but is now growing within Iceland, too.

pews and a dramatic blue ceiling painted with 1,000 gold stars. The altarpiece, which was made in Nottingham, England, came from the old monastery.

Húsavík

To the northeast of Akureyri, **Húsavík** ㉖ occupies a beautiful setting, facing the Víknafjöll mountains over the wide waters of Skjálfandi ('Trembling Bay'). Unsurprisingly, the sea has always been a dominant factor in the town's development, and today people flock here for **whale-watching tours**, for which Húsavík is renowned. The two big operators, North Sailing (www.northsailing.is) and Gentle Giants (www.gentlegiants.is) have between one and 12 sailings per day between April and November: buy tickets from the harbourside huts or book online. In breeding season, they also run trips to two small islands, Lundey and Flatey, to look at puffins.

Down at the harbour is the excellent **Húsavík Whale Museum** (www.whalemuseum.is; charge), Iceland's only museum dedicated to these captivating mammals. It is small, but packed with information to help explain the life-cycle, habits and biology of whales. The

Humpback whales are abundant in Iceland, particularly during the summer months

highlight is the long gallery, where skeletons of whales swim eerily overhead.

Húsavík also has a fine natural history museum, **Safnahúsið** (www.husmus.is; Stórigarður 17; charge), in the same building as the town library. As well as memorabilia from old houses and farms, various old weapons and exhibits of flora and fauna (including a stuffed polar bear captured on the island of Grímsey in 1969), there is a beautifully displayed maritime section that reflects the town's historical dependence on the sea.

Húsavík harbour

The **church** (https://husavikurkirkja.is; Garðarsbraut; free), an impressive wooden building in the shape of a cross, was built in 1906–7 to seat 450 people. The altarpiece features several of the town's residents who posed for a depiction of the resurrection of Lazarus. East of Húsavík, **Þórshöfn** is another place that dates back to the saga times. It grew considerably in the early 20th century during the peak of the herring boom and is still predominantly a fishing town.

Britain's Prince Charles used to favour **Vopnafjörður**, 60km (37 miles) to the southeast, for fishing holidays. He must have arrived by air, as the roads around here are among the worst in Iceland. The locals will tell you that Santa Claus lives on the nearby **Smjörfjöll** – at least he is able to travel freely by sleigh.

Lakes, volcanoes, canyons and falls

Highlights

- **Lake Mývatn**, see page 85
- **Námafjall and Krafla**, see page 88
- **Jökulsárgljúfur**, see page 90

Within easy striking distance of both Akureyri and Húsavík are some of the most impressive geological formations in Iceland. These include two massive waterfalls, Dettifoss and Goðafoss, and Jökulsárgljúfur (see page 90), part of Vatnajökull National Park, which encloses a spectacular canyon with falls of its own. Active

Goðafoss, the 'Waterfall of the Gods'

geothermal areas, craters and bizarre rock formations surround Lake Mývatn, home to a huge variety of ducks. A good road circles the lake close to the shore.

The perfectly proportioned falls at **Goðafoss** ㉗ are easily reached on the drive into the area from the north. The 'Waterfall of the Gods' was so-named because, after returning in the year 1000 from the momentous Alþingi, where he had decided that Iceland should convert to Christianity, law-speaker Þorgeir threw his pagan carvings into its waters.

Lake Mývatn

Despite its name, **Lake Mývatn** ㉘ (Midge Lake) is one of the highlights of any visit to Iceland. Midges and flies love the shallow water at the lake's edge, but they rarely bite, and you can get a hat with netting attached to keep them out of eyes, ears and mouth. The lake, and the **Laxá River** that flows out from the west, are renowned for the variety of **birds** they attract. The area is protected by law, and there are wardens to help visitors enjoy themselves without harming the ecology.

With the peaks of the Krafla caldera and Mt Hverfjall as a backdrop, Lake Mývatn has a serenity that belies the churning geothermal activity just below the surface of the surrounding land. The land around the shore is generally flat, with just a few small hills and pseudocraters, making it ideal territory for gentle hiking or cycling. The Environment Agency of Iceland (www.ust.is) publishes a list of suggested trails. It is worth carrying binoculars because, whether you are an avid birdwatcher or not, the number and variety of ducks and other birdlife here is extraordinary (see box).

Tiny **Reykjahlíð** at the northeast corner of Lake Mývatn has the most amenities, including the tourist office, which can arrange all manner of tours, and a small supermarket. The main sight in the village is its **church**, which is surrounded by hardened lava. A major eruption in 1729 brought lava streaming down from the hills. While it obliterated nearby farmland, it miraculously skirted around the church. Tradition says it was the power of prayer that protected it, although the walls around the cemetery may have helped.

There is plenty of evidence to indicate just how close the geothermal activity is to the surface in this part of Iceland – you may well see gases rising from fissures in the lava around Reykjahlíð. Heading clockwise around the lake, you can sample geothermally-baked *hverabrauð* (see box) at the popular Cowshed Café (Vogafjós; www.vogafjosfarmresort.is), which backs onto a milking shed, so you can watch the working life of the farm while you eat. Slightly set back from the shore road, the hot springs at **Storagjá** can be reached via a ladder and rope. The springs have cooled and become infested with algae, which dissuades most potential swimmers. Nearby, another spring **Grjótagjá** suffers from the opposite problem – it is too hot for most people, but is well worth a look as it's inside a naturally formed cavern in the lava.

Hofdi nature park, on Lake Mývatn

Skirting the edge of the vast tephra cone Hverfjall is enchanting **Dimmuborgir**, a vast, 2,000-year-old field of contorted volcanic pillars, some extending as high as 20 metres (65ft). The helpful visitor centre and café offers guided walks in the area. A

THE DUCKS AND BIRDS OF MÝVATN

Fourteen species of ducks breed on Lake Mývatn and the Laxá River at a density unmatched anywhere else in the world. There are tens of thousands of these birds, all attracted by the warm shallow water, plentiful food and space for nesting.

The most common varieties are the tufted duck, scaup, wigeon, teal and red-breasted merganser. Harlequin ducks live on the river in large numbers, and the common scoter, a diving breed, is widely seen on the west side of the lake. Barrow's goldeneye is only found here and in North America. In the Rockies, where the species originates, the birds lay their eggs in holes in tree trunks; here, they lay them in holes in the lava. The Slavonian grebe builds floating nests close to the shore. The gadwall and red-necked phalarope are common all over the lake.

Other breeds you are likely to see include whooper swans, greylag geese, Arctic tern and the black-headed gull. Ptarmigan are common, and there are several pairs of gyrfalcon nesting here, along with smaller numbers of short-eared owl and merlin.

Sigurgeirs Bird Museum (Fuglasafn Sigurgeirs; www.fuglasafn.is; charge), on Neslandatangi peninsula in the northwestern part of the lake, is great for twitchers. It contains stuffed examples of most Icelandic birds, and has bookable hides at the heart of the action.

viewing platform looks out over the expanse, and visitors can wander among haunting arches, caves and natural tunnels – stick to the paths, as the area is very fragile. The most famous formation is Kirkjan (the Church), a cave whose entrance looks like the window of a Gothic cathedral.

At the southern end of the lake, **Skútustaðir** has a hotel, church, café-restaurant and facilities for horse riding and hiring bikes. Close to the shore there is a collection of pseudocraters, which look like mini volcanoes. In fact they were created when molten lava ran over the marshland. The water below came to the boil and burst through the lava sheet to form cones. Most of

NOTES

The local tradition of underground baking involves mixing rye dough with yeast and molasses, pouring the mixture into old milk cartons and baking them in holes covered by metal sheets for a day. The result is a heavy but moist steam bread known as *hverabrauð*.

the islands in the middle of the lake were formed in the same way.

The Laxá River contains salmon, brown trout and Arctic char, but you'll need to buy an expensive licence if you want to fish. On the eastern side of the lake is the peak of **Vindbelgjarfjall** (530 metres/1,735ft), which can be climbed by a fairly steep path at the back of the mountain for some fantastic views. From here, the road passes through wetlands containing some of the biggest concentrations of birdlife, before returning to Reykjahlíð.

Námafjall and Krafla

The geothermal sights northeast of the lake are ever more amazing. Four kilometres east of Reykjahlíð are the **Mývatn Nature Baths** (Jarðböðin; www.myvatnnaturebaths.is; charge), the north's answer to the Blue Lagoon, though without the crowds. The pool covers 5,000 sq metres (5,980 sq yds) and contains a mix of skin-softening minerals, silicates and micro-organisms. It is the perfect place to sit and soak for an hour or two.

The baths are filled with geothermally heated water from the Bjarnarflag borehole, which taps into a nearby geothermal field. You can admire the sulphurous earth, bubbling mudpots and screaming fumaroles of this high-temperature area at the unearthly Hverir, a little further along the ring road from the baths.

Just past Hverir, road 863 branches north towards the **Krafla caldera** ㉙. There have been eruptions in and around Krafla for much of the past 3,000 years. Nine eruptions between 1977–84 (the so-called Krafla Fires) left a huge field of lava that is still steaming today. The eruptions threatened the **Leirbotn power station**, but stopped just short; you can visit the plant for free most afternoons. Further up the road is a perfectly rounded crater **Viti** ('Hell'), which was formed in 1724 and has since flooded. Its huge size, the strange blue tint to the water and the sheer drop down from the rim makes it an awesome sight. From the Krafla car park you can visit a second crater, **Sjálfskapar Viti**, or 'Home-made Hell', so-called because it was formed when a borehole being drilled for the power station exploded. Fortunately, nobody was killed, but debris from the rig was found for miles around. A well-marked track leads up to the **Leirhnjúkur** lavafield, formed in the mid-18th century

The Grjótagjá pool

and provoked back to life by the Krafla Fires. The path leads past a large and colourful sulphur-encrusted mud-hole, before winding its way around an area of cinder-like mounds and smoking black fissures. Stick to the well-worn paths, for this fragile area's safety and your own: the crust is thin and could give way under a person's weight.

Jökulsárgljúfur

North of Mývatn, **Jökulsárgljúfur**, part of Vatnajökull National Park, straddles part of Iceland's second-longest river, the **Jökulsá á Fjöllum**. More than half the country's plant species are to be found here, but most visitors are drawn by the geology of the area.

Ásbyrgi canyon

Jökulsárgljúfur ('glacier river canyon') is a vast canyon up to 120 metres (395ft) deep and 500 metres (1,640ft) wide. There are numerous waterfalls along its route. The two most impressive, **Dettifoss** (Europe's most powerful falls) and **Selfoss**, are situated at the southern boundary of the park. At the northern tip is the information office where you can acquire details of the area's many walking trails and sights.

NOTES

The Arctic tern is nature's own divebomber. With little provocation, these territorial troublemakers will swoop at intruders, screaming 'kría!' (the bird's name in Icelandic) as they attack. Wear a hat or pull up your hood, and wave a stick or rolled-up newspaper above your head.

From the tourist office, a road leads down towards the great horse-shoe shaped **Ásbyrgi canyon**, a 90 metre (295ft) semicircle of rock flecked with colourful lichens. The first Viking settlers believed that Sleipnir, the god Odin's flying horse, formed the canyon by crashing a giant hoof into the earth. There are several campsites in the park if you want to stay and explore the area.

Eastern Iceland

Highlights

- **Egilsstaðir**, see page 92
- **Lögurinn and Snæfell**, see page 92
- **The Eastfjords**, see page 93

The eastern part of Iceland is one of the least-visited areas of the country and, as a result, has a less well-developed tourist industry. Overall, the region has a quiet, gentle feel, making it pleasant to visit. The East enjoys some of the sunniest weather in the country – and the undulating farmland and rugged coast are ideal for walking.

For the past decade, the region has been at the centre of the greatest environmental debate Iceland has ever known, when it was chosen as the site for an immense dam and aluminium smelter. Construction on the smelter began in Reyðarfjörður in 2004, and was completed by 2008. It transformed the local economy and created scores of new jobs, yet its power is supplied by the Kárahnjúkar Dam, which was built in an environmentally sensitive part of the interior.

Egilsstaðir

With its airport and its pivotal position on the ring road, **Egilsstaðir** ㉚ is the most-visited town in the region. It is not the loveliest of places, but it's a good base for trips to the lakes and mountains to the south of it. A regional museum, **Minjasafn Austurlands** (East Iceland Heritage Museum, Tjarnabraut; www.minjasafn.is; charge), contains exhibits about life in the area. At the northern end of the town is a 25-metre **swimming pool**, which is ideal for relaxing in after a day's walking.

Seyðisfjörður is surrounded by mountains

Lögurinn and Snæfell

The lake of **Lögurinn** runs 30km (19 miles) south from Egilsstaðir, carrying the **Lagarfljót River** from the

Vatnajökull ice cap to the sea. The road around it is rough in places, but, unusually for Iceland, the banks are forested, especially over on the eastern side. The lake is in a deep glacial valley and is said to be home to the **Lagarfljótsormur monster**, a creature not unlike Scotland's Loch Ness monster, although nobody seems to have got close enough to be sure.

NOTES

According to folklore, a young girl found a gold ring and put it in a box with a small snake for safekeeping. When she returned, both the ring and snake had grown. Terrified, she threw them into Lögurinn. The snake grew into the Lagarfljótsormur monster, threatening all who crossed the lake.

The forest at **Hallormsstaður** is the showcase for Iceland's efforts at reforestation after the indiscriminate felling of previous eras. The **arboretum** has examples of around 70 tree species from around the world, all of which are well labelled. There are marked trails here for hikes or horseriding.

At 1,833 metres (6,012ft), **Mt Snæfell** ㉛ is Iceland's highest peak outside the glacial zones. An ancient volcano, Snæfell last erupted some 10,000 years ago. There are marker posts up the western side of the mountain showing the easiest route to the top, although you need to be experienced to tackle the peak itself. However, there are plenty of easier walks on the mountain, and there is the added attraction of the many reindeer that inhabit the area.

The Eastfjords

Although the inlets along the east of Iceland are less dramatic than those in the west and north, they are dotted with lovely little villages, most of which are easily accessible from the ring road. Travellers arriving in Iceland by ferry normally dock at **Seyðisfjörður** ㉜, a pretty little port surrounded by high mountains. A dirt road up to Mt Bjólfur gives spectacular views down over the fjord and the town's brightly painted wooden houses. Although just 665 people live here, Seyðisfjörður has a healthy cultural life: Skaftfell Culture Center stages contemporary art exhibitions; **Bláa kirkjan** (The Blue Church) organises classical concerts on Wednesday evenings from July to mid-August. The town commissioned the unusual sculpture Tvísöngur, perched high in the hills and worth the walk. At the mouth of the 20km (12.42-mile) long fjord, the nature reserve Skálanes (www.skalanes.com), accessible only by boat, on foot or in a 4WD, provides an end-of-the-earth retreat.

A river running through Hallormsstaður forest

In summer, boats (Flóabáturinn Anný; tel: 476 0005 or 853 3004) sail from **Neskaupstaður** around the headland into near-deserted **Mjóifjörður**, past the highest sea-cliff in Iceland.

Eskifjörður is a busy fishing village with a large trawler fleet and a fish-freezing plant. **Sjóminjasafn** (Maritime Museum, Strandgata 39b; www.sjominjasafn.com; charge) is packed with boats, models, nets and fishing equipment. Just south of here, easy walking paths run through the **Hólmanes nature reserve**, known for its birdlife and unusual rock formations. It lies at the foot of the **Hólmatindur** headland, whose summit makes a more challenging climb.

The hills around the small fishing port of **Reyðarfjörður** have been worn flat by the now-vanished glaciers. The town was a naval base during World War II, and there is a museum, **Stríðsárasafnið** (Icelandic Wartime Museum, Austurvegur; http://stridsarasafn.fjardabyggd.is; charge), which documents the billeting of 3,000 Allied soldiers here.

A trip out from **Djúpivogur** to the uninhabited island of **Papey**, 'Monk's Island', reveals Iceland's smallest church, little bigger than a hencoop, which is chained to the ground to prevent it blowing away. Today the island is a nature reserve, home to seabirds (including 30,000 puffin pairs) and a large breeding colony of eider ducks.

The Interior

Highlights

- **Askja and Herðubreið**, see page 96
- **The Sprengisandur Route**, see page 96
- **The Kjölur Route**, see page 98

Iceland's barren interior – a place so desolate that the Apollo astronauts came here to train for their moon landing – can be crossed by two main north–south routes; Sprengisandur (F26) and Kjölur (F35, also known as the Kjalvegur), both of which are open only once the snow has melted in summer. Some of the more minor routes remain closed throughout the summer if conditions are poor. East of Mývatn, the F88 eventually splits into several highland 'dead-ends': however, the final destinations – the distinctive mountain Herðubreið, the Askja caldera and the Kverkfjöll ice caves – are stunning. The weather is generally very unpredictable in the interior, so always be prepared for the worst.

Camping is the only form of accommodation, apart from a few huts operated by Ferðafélag Íslands (Iceland Touring Association; www.fi.is), plus the Hrauneyjar motel (www.hrauneyjar.is) and Kiðagil guesthouse (www.kidagil.is) at either end of the Sprengisandur route. Visitors without transport can take advantage of the scheduled buses that run between Reykjavík and Lake Mývatn via Sprengisandur and between Reykjavík and Akureyri via the Kjölur route. Private tour operators can take you from Akureyri and Mývatn to Herðubreið, Askja and Kverkfjöll.

Askja and Herðubreið

From Mývatn, the F88 crosses a moonlike plateau and several glacial streams before reaching the distinctive table mountain Herðubreið, known as the queen of Iceland's mountains, and the flower-filled nature reserve Herðubreiðarlindir. The F88 turns into the F910, with one branch bumping on to the stunning **Askja caldera** ㉝, the scene of epic eruptions in 1874–5 when vents under lake Öskjuvatn threw out two billion cubic metres of ash. On the edge of the lake, the crater Víti (Hell) contains milky-blue water that is still warm from the last eruption in 1961 – bring a swimsuit. The other branch heads south, eventually petering out at the mighty icecap Vatnajökull: a steep hike brings you to spectacular ice caves inside the Kverkfjöll glacier. Further south is the **Holuhraun lava field**, formed during an eruption of the Bardarbunga volcano, which lasted from August 2014 to February 2015.

The Sprengisandur Route

The second main crossing through the interior, the Sprengisandur route, runs from the Bárðardalur Valley between Akureyri and Lake Mývatn to Þjórsá, east of Selfoss. It is accessible by 4WD only and covers some of the most desolate ground in the country.

There are three main ways to reach the start of the route proper, all of which converge at or near Laugafell at the edge of the

Sprengisandur. The most easterly way (route 842 then F26) heads through the Bárðardalur Valley via two waterfalls; Goðafoss and the basalt Aldeyjarfoss. A more central route (F821) goes from the end of the Eyjafjörður Valley, past the former farm/weather station at Nýibær, towards Laugafell. The third, most westerly, route (F752) meanders through the Vesturdalur Valley from Skagafjörður.

At Laugafell, on a ridge leading northwest from the mountain of the same name, there are several warm springs, a warm bathing pool and a tourist hut. Nearby, the gravel expanse of the Sprengisandur begins with magnificent vistas east to Vatnajökull and the smaller Tungnafellsjökull and west to Hofsjökull. A number of river crossings later, the blue tongues of glaciers come into view.

Landmannalaugar's rhyolitic hills

At Nýidalur, close to the geographical centre of Iceland, is a small campsite, on the only patch of green in the area, and several huts. The next stop on the route is shortly after the mountain of Kistualda (790m/2,600ft). The dusty track south to **Þórisvatn** ❸❹, Iceland's second largest lake, continues the landscape of glaciers and black gravel plains. Just beyond the lake is the tiny settlement of Hrauneyjafoss, where there is a petrol station, coffee-shop and small guesthouse.

Next is **Landmannalaugar** ❸❺, part of the Fjallabak Nature Reserve and a good base for the many walks in the area (there are camping and hut facilities here). Landmannalaugar's spectacular rhyolitic hills are bright yellow, green and red, dotted with deep blue lakes. There are hot springs here, and steam rises from every corner of the valley.

Geothermal spring at Hveravellir

From Landmannalaugar, it is possible either to head southwestwards to meet the ring road near the south coast, or southeast to Bláfjall and the coast.

The Kjölur Route

Comparatively straightforward to drive, the Kjölur is the most popular crossing through the central highlands. This is the only route through the interior that travellers could consider making in a normal car, as all the rivers are bridged.

However, rental cars are not insured for the route; and it is still strongly advised to travel by 4WD.

Based on an ancient byway used in saga times, the route runs from Gullfoss to the Blöndudalur Valley, passing between the Langjökull and Hofsjökull ice-caps. Behind Gullfoss, the River Hvítá flows out of Hvítárvatn, a glacial lake at the foot of Langjökull. From the main route you should be able to see the lake and its glacial spurs, which extend up to its shores.

Bathing in natural hot springs

The route soon reaches its highest point (just over 670 metres/2,200ft), where a memorial stone commemorates the achievements of Geir Zoëga, an engineer who was for many years in charge of building Iceland's roads.

At the centre of the Kjölur plateau is **Hveravellir** 36, an area of intense geothermal activity, with hot springs, a hot pool where you can bathe, camping facilities and good overnight huts. Also at Hveravellir is a modest stone shelter where the bandit Fjalla Eyvindur and his wife Halla spent a whole winter in hiding in the 18th century.

The northern section of the route, which is less attractive, follows a track through the reservoir basin created for Blönduvirkjun hydroelectric power station. After crossing the Blandá River at about halfway between Blönduós and Varmahlíð, you will reach the Blöndudalur Valley and then the ring road.

Enjoying the water in the Eastfjords

Things to do

Outdoor activities

There is a great deal on offer for exploring the great outdoors in Iceland, from gentle hikes and horse-riding excursions to more demanding pursuits such as ice-climbing and white-water rafting.

Walking and Hiking

There are hiking trails throughout Iceland to suit every level. The more ambitious routes require some previous experience and a high level of fitness. The weather can change unexpectedly and if you can't read a map and a compass properly then don't attempt the hikes that take you away from populated areas.

The two organisations that provide hiking information, details of mountain huts for overnight stays, as well as guided hikes are: **Ferðafélag Íslands** (Iceland Touring Association, Mörkin 6, 108 Reykjavík, www.fi.is) and **Útivist** (Borgartúni 3, 105 Reykjavík, www.utivist.is). Tourist offices can provide maps and local contacts for guides.

By far the best months for hiking are June, July and August, when the weather is relatively warm, and visibility is at its best. Beginners could start with some of the excellent walking paths around Reykjavík: the longest runs right round the headland, passing Grótta lighthouse, Seltjarnarnes golf club and Nauthólsvík geothermal beach, before heading 10km (6 miles) east inland to the Heiðmörk conservation area. Ask the tourist office for further information.

Every part of the country has its trails. Some of the best areas for walking and hiking include:

Þingvellir (Thingvellir) National Park. Marked trails around historic sites and lakes. One option is a full-day hike up Mt Armannsfell.

Landmannalaugar–Þórsmörk Trail. Experienced walkers will love Iceland's best-known hike, the 53km (33 miles) 'Laugavegurinn'. It can be extended to reach Skógar, a further 25km (15.5 miles) to the south.

Snæfellsnes Peninsula. A rugged and often wet area. Ascent of the glacier for experienced hikers.

Hornstrandir. One of the wildest and most isolated parts of the country, suitable for the experienced only.

Lake Mývatn. Flat and gentle routes amid terrific scenery.

Jökulsárgljúfur (Vatnajökull National Park). Well-marked trails at all levels, taking from a few hours to four days.

Skaftafell (Vatnajökull National Park). Trails at different levels, from a well-trodden glacier path to the unmarked 24km (15-mile) round-trip to Kjós.

Mt Snæfell. Demanding hikes from Egilsstaðir along the lake and up the mountain. An 80km (50-mile) trail runs from Snæfell to Stafafell, in the Lónsöræfi wilderness area.

Hikes into the **interior**, where there are few roads and no villages, can be very tough but rewarding. The mighty rivers make many of the routes and tracks impassable by foot, but the **F35 Kjölur track** is passable in summer without a vehicle. Always seek advice from one of the touring organisations (see page 101) before setting off.

Horse Riding

Icelandic horses are descended from the sturdy breed brought over by the Vikings. They can be hired, with or without guides, from farms and activity centres all over Iceland. Treks can be as short as an hour, or as long as 10 days, with accommodation in tents or huts. If you are bringing your own equipment or clothing it must be disinfected on arrival. Contact local tourist offices for details of tour providers, or see the Hey Iceland website (www.heyiceland.is) for a list of farms offering horse-riding tours and holidays. The magazine *Eíðfaxi International* (https://eidfaxi.is/en) is published for Icelandic horse lovers worldwide.

Fishing

Spectacular hiking country

Salmon and trout fishing in Iceland have an international reputation, both for superb runs of fish and the crystal-clear waters. For salmon, the season is from the third week of May until mid-September, with fishing permitted for 105 days within that period; and for trout it's April/May until late September/October, depending on the location. Excellent fishing is available but at a very high price, which varies according to river and facilities available. The very cheapest salmon permits start at around ISK60,000 per rod per day in peak season, usually as part of a (minimum) three-day package. The other snag is that most rivers have to be booked months, if not years, in advance. Iceland's waters are disease-free, so all equipment coming into the country, including waders and boots, must be disinfected. For further information contact the **Federation of Icelandic River Owners** (Bændahöllin, Hagatorg, 107 Reykjavík, www.angling.is).

Birdwatching

The quantity and variety of bird life in Iceland really has to be seen to be believed: the country is home to some of the largest breeding colonies in the world. The best locations are:

Látrabjarg in the West Fjords: the largest bird cliff in Europe.

Heimaey: once the site of Iceland's largest puffin colony, although numbers are in sharp decline. Other puffin-packed places include Lundey Island near Reykjavík; around the cliffs at Vík; at Borgarfjörður Eystri.
Lake Mývatn in the north: there are more species of breeding ducks here than anywhere in Europe.
Dyrhólaey Cliffs: here and elsewhere along the south coast has Arctic tern as well as the world's largest skua colony.
The **Icelandic Society for the Protection of Birds (Fuglaverndarfélag Íslands)** can be contacted at Hverfisgata 105, 101 Reykjavik, http://fuglavernd.is.

Ice-climbing and Glacier Walks

In summer, guided day-walks on the glaciers from Skaftafell (part of Vatnajökull National Park) can be arranged with two companies based at the visitor centre; the **Icelandic Mountain Guides** (www.mountainguides.is) and the **Glacier Guides** (www.

ICELAND'S BIRDLIFE

Iceland is renowned for its birdlife, hosting over 370 (mostly migratory) species. Sea-birds make up the majority – some of the world's largest breeding colonies of gannets, guillemots, razorbills, storm-petrels, arctic skuas, arctic terns and puffins are found here – although there has been a worrying crash in the number of breeding pairs. There are also large numbers of waders and wildfowl. Many species are strictly protected by law.

The lesser black-backed gull is the first migrant to arrive, in February/March, but the locals regard the arrival of the golden plover in April as the start of spring. The best time to go birdwatching is in early summer. Many breeds pass through during the last two weeks of May on their way north to Greenland. In early June the resident breeding species begin their mating rituals. It is important not to disturb the birds at this time. In the second half of June the chicks start to hatch and by mid-August they are leaving the nest.

glacierguides.is). **Local Guide** (www.localguide.is) offers private tours on various glaciers within the national park. They and the Icelandic Mountain Guides also offer more ambitious winter expeditions, including ice climbing and ascents of Iceland's highest peak Hvannadalshnúkur – see the websites for details.

Ice-climbing

Glacier tours with **snowmobiles** are a fun (if noisy!) way to see the ice close up. Several companies run trips on to the Vatnajökull glacier in the southeast, Snæfellsjökull in the west, and Langjökull in the southwest, close to the sights of the Golden Circle. Contact local tourist offices for details.

Snow Sports

You probably wouldn't come to Iceland just for the **downhill skiing** and **snowboarding**, although they are popular diversions for Icelanders making the best of the dark northern winter. On clear, calm weekends in March and April, the whole of Reykjavík seems to head out of town to the Bláfjöll skiing area (www.skidasvaedi.is), where there are 14 busy lifts and a cafe. A day pass costs a reasonable ISK6,150, and boot and ski hire around ISK7,250. Scheduled buses depart from the Mjódd bus terminal on the eastern outskirts of Reykjavík once a day. There are also good slopes at Akureyri (www.hlidarfjall.is).

Several tour operators run **cross-country skiing** trips in spring: check with Ferðafélag and Útivist (see page 101), or with Ice Guide and the Icelandic Mountain Guides (see page 104).

Dog-sledding Iceland (www.dogsledding.is) run excursions on Langjökull glacier in the southwest, snow conditions permitting.

White-Water Rafting

Visitors can shoot the rapids on three of Iceland's glacial rivers between May and mid-September. The fairly gentle Hvítá river is easily accessed on day trips from Reykjavík. However, if you're heading north, the remote Jökulsá Vestari and Jökulsá Austari, near Varmahlíð in Skagafjörður, should be your first choice. The western branch is suitable for families, while the eastern river is a wilder ride. For details (including minimum ages), contact Arctic Rafting, (www.arcticrafting.com).

Speeding on the Skálafellsjökull

Swimming

More than just a sport in Iceland, swimming is a social activity for all the family, and there are geothermally heated pools in most towns and many villages – see www.swimminginiceland.com for a full list. If you want to do serious lengths, the best pool in Reykjavík is at Laugardalur on Sundlaugavegur (tel: 411 5100). It has a 50 metre

Iceland offers great opportunities for whale-watching

(160ft) pool, three hot pots, a Jacuzzi, steam room, sun lamps and waterslide.

Whale-Watching

Whale-watching started in Iceland in 1995, but since then the number of companies offering tours has been increasing. There is usually a good chance of seeing something – most likely harbour porpoises and white-beaked dolphins. Of the larger species, the minke whale is most common, although humpbacks, fin and even blue whales are spotted from time to time.

Húsavík, with its excellent Whale Museum, is acknowledged as Iceland's 'whale-watching capital', but there are also departures from Reykjavík, Akureyri, Bíldudalur, Dalvík, Heimaey and Ólafsvík. However, you don't have to be on a boat to see whales

– just looking out to sea might reveal a whale's back breaking the surface.

Cycling

The unmade roads and high winds in much of Iceland can make cycle touring a challenge, to say the least. Off-road cycling is prohibited to help protect the environment.

The **Icelandic Mountain Bike Club** (Íslenski Fjallhjólaklúbburinn, Brekkustíg 2, 101 Reykjavík, www.fjallahjolaklubburinn.is) is a great source of advice and has suggested itineraries.

Golf

With 65 courses, golf is thriving in Iceland. Most courses have just nine holes, however there are seventeen 18-hole courses including those in: Reykjavík (Grafarholt and Korpa), Hafnarfjörður (Keilir), Garðabær (Oddur), Hella, Keflavík (Suðurnes), Vestmannaeyjar and Akureyri. For further information contact the **Golf Federation of Iceland** (Golfsamband Íslands, Engjavegur 6, 104 Reykjavík, http://golficeland.org). The major golfing event in Iceland is the Arctic Open, which takes place in June each year and is open to professional and amateur golfers alike. The event's host is the **Akureyri Golf Club** (Eikarlundur 18, www.arcticopen.is).

Activities for children

Icelanders try to involve children in almost all their sporting and cultural activities. Swimming and horse riding are particularly popular with local children, and families gather in large numbers at weekends to feed the ducks and geese at Tjörnin in front of City Hall.

The pool at Laugardalur (see page 106) has a huge 85m (280ft) waterslide and a children's pool. At the same site, Reykjavík's Zoo and Family Park (www.mu.is; charge) is always a hit with small kids, and when they tire of looking at the seals, foxes, reindeer, horses, cows and pigs, they can head for the Family Park and climb a replica Viking ship and cross a man-made lake on a raft. There is a large grill that can be used free of charge for barbecuing. The seals are fed twice a day.

For older children there are two bowling rinks (keiluhöllin, http://keiluhollin.is; charge) at Öskjuhlíð near Perlan, and in the Egilshöll sports facility in the suburb of Grafarvogur.

Golf on the Westman Islands

Culture

While outdoor adventures are Iceland's biggest draw, there is also much for culture vultures, and particularly those interested in history, to absorb here. Reykjavík has by far the country's most thriving **cultural** scene, which is documented in *What's On in Reykjavík* and local papers, which list the latest music, dance and theatre performances.

The city's dazzling harbour concert hall, Harpa, is home to both the Icelandic Opera and the internationally acclaimed Iceland Symphony Orchestra, which perform there from September to mid-June. Outside those months, there is a packed summer programme of pop, rock and classical music events, both in and outside of Reykjavík – see www.icelandmusic.is for details.

Across Iceland, though, there are fantastic museums which tell the fascinating story of the country's long and unique history. These range from Reykholt's Snorrastofa, a centre dedicated to the legendary saga writer and politician Snorri Sturluson, to Akureyri's

Reykjavík has a good selection of stylish bars

Minjasafnið á Akureyri (Municipal Museum), which tells the story of Iceland's modest second city through an exhibition of everyday items.

Nightlife

Reykjavík is renowned for its lively weekend nightlife, when jolly drinkers cram into the city's tiny, offbeat and oh-so-cool bars for shouted conversations, flowing booze, spontaneous musical happenings and dancing. In the summertime in particular, Icelanders make the most of the endless sunlight to dance until dawn – it can often feel like nobody ever goes to bed in Reykjavík in midsummer. A popular tradition is the *runtur*, which translates as 'round tour' (pub crawl).

There are dozens of very welcoming bars and cafés for a drink or light meal during the evening, but the serious clubbing doesn't start until well after midnight – people usually drink at home before going out to party, as bar prices are so high. Icelanders tend to dress up a bit to go out, and there can be long queues outside the most fashionable places on Friday and Saturday.

Clubs and pubs open and close in Reykjavík all the time, so it's worth asking around to find out where the newest and most fashionable places are; or check out the free newspaper the *Reykjavík Grapevine* (www.grapevine.is), which takes its gigs and nightlife seriously.

Shopping

This is not a cheap destination by the standards of most travellers, and Icelandic products are marketed at those who believe in paying for quality and smart design. However, the unusual books, music and food on offer, plus beautifully made homeware, clothing and jewellery, will have you reaching for your credit card. In the centre of Reykjavík, most of the tourist shops are in and around Hafnarstræti and Austurstræti, though Laugavegur, leading out of the centre, is home to the majority of the fashion shops. Skólavörðustígur, which branches off Laugavegur at a sharp diagonal, is good for quirky gifts and crafts. In the suburbs are two large malls, Smáralind (www.smaralind.is) and Kringlan (www.kringlan.is), which house most of the usual European high-street chain stores. The biggest, Kringlan, has over 150 shops and food outlets and is easy to reach – it's just a 15-minute bus-ride from the city centre.

For **souvenirs** try Icelandic woollen sweaters, gloves, scarves and hats. Most are produced by small workshops and come in

TAX-FREE SHOPPING

On leaving Iceland, you can get a refund of the VAT (Value Added Tax) paid on goods over ISK6,000. The shop assistant will fill out a Tax Free form – keep this safe, along with your purchase receipt. For an immediate refund, take the form to the tax refund points (be prepared to queue) at the Kringlan or Smáralind shopping malls, Reykjavík tourist office, or the counters in the BSÍ bus station, the airport or the Skarfabakki cruise-ship service centre. Otherwise you can get a refund later by post.

If the total is more than ISK5,000 for any one item, you will have to show the goods to customs on your way out of the country, and obtain a customs stamp before you can claim your refund. This does not apply for woollen goods. This scheme can save you up to 15 percent on the price of many items.

all shapes, sizes and colours. The Handknitting Association of Iceland's shops (Handþrjónasamband Íslands, Skólavörðustigur 19 & Laugavegur 64, http://handknit.is) have a wide selection. Skólavörðustigur has a number of **art** galleries selling some excellent local work, as well as shops selling the best of Icelandic **design**. Duvets, quilts and other bedcovers are also very good quality, although those filled with locally gathered eider down can be expensive.

For traditional **Icelandic music**, try the album Íslensk alþýðulög (Icelandic Folk Songs). There are also fine classical recordings by the Iceland Symphony Orchestra, particularly of works by the late composer Jón Leifs. Of course, Björk and Sigur Rós are Iceland's biggest musical exports, but the modern music scene is ever-changing and new bands appear all the time.

Smoked salmon, roe caviar, dried fish and *skyr*, a delicious Icelandic yoghurt, are good food buys, but be aware of the import restrictions.

Festivals and events

Precise dates change from year to year. Check with tourist offices.

6 January Twelfth Night, marked with songs, bonfires and fireworks.

February Þorrablót. The half-way point of winter, this festival involves eating delicacies including lambs' heads and testicles, and cured shark.

Early February Festival of Lights. Reykjavík's winter festival with arts and cultural events.

Early March. Food & Fun Festival (www.foodandfun.is). A week-long culinary feast, attracting the best chiefs from the US and Europe who then team up with local restaurants to create original yet affordable menus.

1st Thursday after April 18th The First Day of Summer. Marked by parades, sports events and the giving of summer-themed gifts.

1st Sunday in June Festival of the Sea. Celebrations in all coastal communities with sports and dances.

17 June National Day. Formal ceremonies in the morning and partying and fairs all afternoon and evening.

May/June Reykjavík Arts Festival (www.listahatid.is/en). A biannual two-week celebration of music, theatre, art and dance.

Early July (biannual) Landsmót National Horse Show (www.landsmot.is), held in different towns.

Woollen goods on display

1st Monday in August Summer Bank Holiday. A long weekend for all Icelanders, with open-air pop festivals around the country.

August. Reykjavík Jazz Festival (http://reykjavikjazz.is). An annual jazz feast with international stars.

September/October Reykjavík Film Festival (www.riff.is). A 10-day extravaganza featuring both Icelandic and international movies.

Early November Iceland Airwaves (www.icelandairwaves.is). A five-day tidal-wave of international indie/pop/rock.

23 December St Þórláksmessa. Feast-day of Iceland's patron saint; the high point of the pre-Christmas celebrations.

31 December New Year's Eve. A satirical revue is shown on television, followed by outdoor parties with bonfires and fireworks that continue all through the night.

Food and drink

Iceland is not a foodie destination on the level of its Nordic neighbours, but dining out here, or in Reykjavík at least, has undergone tremendous changes in the past 30 years.

Iceland was effectively cut off from the rest of Europe for centuries, and, with very little in the way of food imports, no Icelandic *haute cuisine* developed. The population depended on what they could catch or grow themselves, making do with a diet based almost entirely on fish, lamb and vegetables such as potatoes. Various methods were devised to preserve the food so it could be used for months after it was caught. Meat was smoked, salted and pickled. Fish would be hung out and dried, or smoked in dung or salted, or even buried. You will still occasionally see fish-drying racks on the hillsides as you drive around the country.

ETIQUETTE AND MEALTIMES

Icelanders tend to have their main meal in the middle of the day and this is also when you can find some of the better priced all-inclusive menus (often restricted to around noon–2.30pm). In Reykjavík and many of the larger towns, restaurants tend to be open all day from about 11.30am until 11pm (later at weekends), so you don't have to be too organised about when you eat. In some smaller places, cafés and restaurants shut at about 2.30pm and reopen around 7pm. They close any time after 10pm, so it's always a good idea to check their opening times before planning your evening. Breakfast hours are relaxed, so you don't usually have to be up too early to fit in with them.

Icelandic mealtime etiquette mirrors that of other northern European nations. The fork is held in the left hand and the knife in the right, dinner usually begins between 7 and 8pm, and service charges are included in your bill, so additional tipping is not expected.

Fresh fish is a staple in Iceland

Things are slowly becoming more cosmopolitan, in Reykjavík at least. There are now Indian and French restaurants, alongside a recent slew of establishments consciously harking back to the country's 'old' cuisine, with dishes like grilled puffin and whale which may be controversial with some visitors.

Where to Eat

The restaurant scene has been hit by a great wave of energy, enthusiasm and experimentation, and dining out in Reykjavík is consequently a real treat – and certainly a far cry from the 1980s, when beer was illegal and foreign influence was unheard of. Prices are not low in Iceland's better restaurants – but, in top restaurants like Apotek and Sjávargrillið, you are paying for excellent meals made with high-quality ingredients.

Outside of the restaurant scene, there is not a great deal to speak of – in most towns, the dining options comprise basic restaurants and cafes, serving mostly Icelandic foods alongside well-established international favourites like hamburgers and, in particular, pizzas. Iceland has so far remained largely immune to the international craze for 'global street food' halls, and the only food trucks to speak of for the most part are those selling *pylsur*, the classic Icelandic hot dog. Made from a combination of beef, pork and lamb, these delicious sandwiches are the classic Icelandic street food experience, and you mustn't leave without trying at least one.

Top Ten Things to Try

1. Fish

Fish is plentiful and cheap, so many meals, from breakfast onwards, will include it in some form. Wind-dried cod or haddock, *harðfiskur*, is a popular snack. It is torn into strips, tenderised and eaten with butter, accompanied with a glass of milk or maybe something stronger. Fresh seafood is excellent, too. Icelandic cod, halibut, turbot and monkfish, for example, are juicy and succulent. Salmon and trout from the rivers are large and relatively inexpensive, as is char, a species of trout that is found all over Iceland. Smoked salmon and gravadlax (smoked salmon marinated with herbs) are both of very high quality.

NOTES

Ice-covered land and frozen seas forced Icelanders to preserve their fish and meat, so it could be stored and eaten throughout winter.

2. Fermented shark

One of Iceland's most notorious food rituals is the ceremonious intake of rotten shark (*hákarl*) and schnapps. After being buried for three months or more, shark

Café Riis in Holmavík serves up delicious meals

becomes acrid and ammoniac; rubbery and rotten, it is washed down in small cubes with ample quantities of the Icelandic spirit, *brennivín*.

3. Lamb

The other Icelandic staple beside fish is lamb. Sheep farms on the island are small, and the flocks are allowed to graze wild in the highlands, where they eat herbs as well as grass. As a result, the meat has quite a gamey flavour.

As with fish, lamb was traditionally smoked to produce *hangikjöt*, which is eaten hot or cold.

4. Offal

Nothing was ever allowed to go to waste in winter in Iceland, and dishes made of sheep's offal are still produced. *Slátur* (literally 'slaughter') is a haggis-like dish made from all manner of left-overs, pressed into cakes, pickled in whey and cooked in stomach lining. Alternatively *svið* are boiled and singed sheep's heads, minus the brains, that are eaten either fresh or pickled. The meat is sometimes then taken off the bone and pressed to produce *sviðasulta*. A real delicacy, served on special occasions, is *súrsaðir hrútspungar* (pickled rams' testicles).

5. Game

A limited amount of game finds its way onto the dinner plate. Reindeer from the east of the country is similar to venison. Ptarmigan is a grouse-like bird and a favourite at Christmas time. Icelanders are quite happy to eat those cute little puffins too; the bird is frequently smoked and produces quite a dark, rich meat.

Fermented shark

6. Skyr

One delicious treat is *skyr*, a yoghurt-type dish made of pasteurised skimmed milk and live bacteria; it's often mixed with fruit flavouring and is high in calcium and low in calories. When you get a packed lunch provided ahead of a long hike, you'll often find skyr included in a pouch drink form – a tasty and refreshing protein boost.

7. Rye Bread

Bread, often made with rye, is a normal accompaniment to any meal. It may be baked in underground ovens in the naturally hot earth to produce *hverabrauð* ('steam bread'). Rye pancakes, known as *flatkaka*, also go well with smoked salmon and other smorgasbord-type toppings.

8. Coffee

Coffee is the national drink of Iceland, consumed from early morning to late at night, at home, at work or even walking down the street. Refills are usually included if you buy a cup of standard coffee in a café, and some petrol stations have a free jug on the counter for their petrol-buying customers. Classic drip-filtered rocket-fuel is supplemented countrywide by espressos, cappuccinos, macchiatos and lattes.

9. Beer

Drinking beer was illegal in Iceland from 1915–89. Its reintroduction – on 1 March 1989 – is celebrated annually as Bjórdagurinn (Beer Day), and in the decades since, Icelanders have taken to beer-drinking with gusto. There are now dozens of nationally available Icelandic lagers, with the most common brands including Kaldi, Gull, and Viking. An increasing number of microbreweries specialising in craft beers are also popping up, particularly in Rekjyavík.

10. Brennivín

Icelandic spirits, on the other hand, are both strong and tasty. *Brennivín* ('burnt wine') is a schnapps distilled from potatoes and flavoured with caraway seeds. Its nickname is 'Black Death', which gives an idea of its strength. A good variant is *Hvannarótar*, which is flavoured with angelica. *Brennivín* is also commonly served alongside *hákarl* (fermented shark) – it's one of the few things that can mask the overwhelming flavour of rotten fish.

Menu reader

Gætum við/get ég fengið... Could we/I have...

Basics

ávextir fruit
bakað baked
baunir peas, beans
brauð bread
grilluð grilled
grænmeti vegetables
hrísgrjón rice
kartöflur potatoes
laukur onion
ostar cheeses
reykt smoked
salat salad
smjör butter
smárettir snacks
soðið boiled
steikt fried
súpa soup
sveppur mushroom

Drinks

appelsínusafi orange juice
bjór beer
kaffi coffee
mjólk milk
te tea
vatn water
vín wine
(hrauðvín) (red)
(hvítvín) (white)

Fiskur (Fish)

bleikja char
hörpuskel scallop
humar lobster
lax salmon
lúða halibut
rauðspretta plaice
sandhverfa turbot
síld herring
silungur trout
skötuselur monkfish
steinbítur catfish
ýsa haddock
rækja shrimp
þorskur cod

Kjöt (Meat)

Kjúklingur chicken
Lambakjöt lamb
Lambakótelettur lamb chop
lundi puffin
nautakjöt beef
nautalundir beef fillet
nautasteik beef steak
önd duck
skinka ham
svínakjöt pork
lítið steikt rare
miðlungs steikt medium
vel steikt well done

Places to eat

We have used the following symbols to give an idea of the price for a three-course meal for one, excluding wine:
$$$$ = over ISK12,000
$$$ = ISK6,000–12,000
$$ = ISK3,000–6,000
$ = below ISK3,000

Reykjavík

Apotek Austurstraeti 16, https://apotekrestaurant.is. Offering a mix of Icelandic and European cuisine, Apotek is on the chic side and tends to be packed; booking is recommended. The tasting menu is particularly good for those who want to try a bit of everything. Dishes are designed to be shared. **$$$$**

Austur India Fjélagið Hverfisgata 56, http://austurindia.is. Indian spices and Icelandic ingredients turn out to be a perfect match: celebrate the happy marriage at this great little restaurant. The menu favours cuisine from the northwest of India in the form of its succulent tandoori dishes, along with turmeric, tamarind and ginger-flavoured delights from other regions. **$$$**

Bastard Brew & Food Vegamótastígur 4, www.bastard.is. Make a bee-line for this brewery to try the craft beer that is brewed right here on the premises; they also have other local beers on tap. There are plenty of ap-petizers to go with the beer as well as simple, filling dishes such as fish or meat of the day or hamburger of the month. **$$$**

Borg Restaurant Pósthússtræti 11, https://borgrestaurant.is. Situated on the ground floor of Hotel Borg, this is a very elegant place surrounded by Art Deco splendour. Imagine that you are back in the 1930s – except, of course, for the distinctly modern prices. The menu is eclectic and includes delights such as smoked puffin breast in a beetroot sauce. **$$$$**

Dill Laugavegur 59, http://dillrestaurant.is. A gourmet's delight, this elegant Scandinavian restaurant specialises in local, organic ingredients cooked in contemporary 'Nordic Kitchen' style. It has even earned a Michelin star. Prepare yourself for mouthwatering dishes such as smoked haddock with blue mussels, reindeer with blueberry sauce, and almond cake with cinnamon ice-cream. **$$$$**

Duck and Rose Austurstræti 14, www.duckandrose.is. A Reykjavík classic, this cosy little cafe overlooking Austurvöllur square and the Parliament Buildings has been here as long as anyone can remember, albeit under a different name. Parisian in style and feel, this is a good choice for a light lunch and a good cup of coffee. In summer there is outdoor seating. **$$**

Icelandic Fish & Chips Tryggvagata 11, www.fishandchips.is. The fish and chips here are given a healthy spin, made with organic potatoes and the freshest quality fish. No wheat or sugar is used in the fish batter, the chips are roasted rather than deep-fried, and the unusual selection of dressings is made using low-fat, yoghurt-like *skyr*. It does a roaring trade in takeaways, too. **$$**

Islenskí Barinn Ingólfsstræti 1a, https://islenskibarinn.is. If you're interested in sampling some of the more distinctive Icelandic delicacies, head to this atmospheric restaurant-bar, which reaches just the right amount of rowdiness at the weekend. Dishes include grilled puffin crumpet, sheep's head, and the infamous *hákarl* (fermented shark). **$$**

Jómfrúin Lækjargata 4, www.jomfruin.is. An excellent choice for lunch, when the restaurant is full of homesick Danes. A seemingly endless choice of filling Danish-style open sandwiches. Choose carefully and lunch need not cost more than ISK4,000. **$**

Kaffivagninn Grandagarði 10, http://kaffivagninn.is. Open since 1935, this is arguably the oldest restaurant in Reykjavik. Located near the harbour, it boasts fantastic views. The menu is short, but has an excellent choice of Scandinavian and Icelandic meals. Good place for breakfast or Sunday brunch. **$$**

Kol Restaurant Skólavörðustígur 40, http://kolrestaurant.is. This small, cosy venue offers a great selection of fish and meat dishes that are prepared using local ingredients. The dinner tasting and gourmet menus are excellent, but expensive; the set lunch menu won't exceed ISK5,000. There are also vegetarian options. **$$$**

Old Iceland Laugavegur 72, https://oldiceland.is. A small, family run restaurant which specializes in simple, historic recipes: meat soup with lamb and vegetables, or fillet of cod with garlic mash, carrots and parsnips. **$$$**

Salka Valka Kitchen Skólavörðustígur 23, https://salkakitchen.com. Named after Halldór Laxness' novel, this a charming and colourful restaurant where you'll feel right at home. Their smoked salmon and herring appetizers are a must. There are tables outside for summer and good vegan options. It gets busy at times, so it's advisable to book ahead. **$$$**

Sjávargrillið Bergstaðastræti 37, https://sjavargrillid.is. Sjávargrillið is one of Reykjavík's finest restaurants, with a menu of exquisitely sourced and presented Icelandic cuisine. The award-winning chef uses fresh local produce, with a particular emphasis on seafood, and presents the dishes with creativity and some international touches. The menu is particularly celebrated for its lobster soup and langoustine tacos. **$$$$**

Thrír Frakkar Baldursgata 14, http://3frakkar.is. This French-style bistro leans towards seafood and traditional Icelandic game: whale steak in pepper sauce, horse tenderloin with mushrooms and *plokkfiskur* (a creamy fish and potato stew). **$$$**

South and Southeast

Kaffi Krús Austurvegur 7, Selfoss, www.kaffikrus.is. Selfoss is hardly the loveliest Icelandic town, but it's the nearest large settlement to the Golden Circle. Break up your sightseeing with lunch at this warm, welcoming bistro, set in a creaky-floored old wooden house. **$$**

Lava Restaurant Blue Lagoon, Grindavík, www.bluelagoon.com. Eat overlooking the thermal spa at this world-famous spot. The menu uses fish brought ashore at the nearby harbour in a variety of international dishes including bouillabaisse and curried cod. **$$$$**

Við Fjöruborðið Eyrarbraut 3a, Stokkseyri, www.fjorubordid.is. Reykjavík residents drive the 70km (40 miles) to Stokkseyri simply to dine at Við Fjöruborðið. This atmospheric seaside restaurant specialises in lobster, and is said to have the best lobster soup in Iceland. **$$$**

East and Northeast

Bautinn Hafnarstræti 92, Akureyri, www.bautinn.is. A good choice in the centre of Akureyri for burgers, pizzas, no-nonsense fry-ups and simple meat and fish dishes. **$$**

Gamli Bærinn Beside Hotel Reynihlíð, Mývatn, www.icelandhotelcollectionbyberjaya.com. The building, which dates from 1912, is by the architect who designed Reykjavík's Parliament. The place is now a delightful little restaurant, where char soup is served and live jazz is played. **$$**

Rub 23 Kaupvangsstræti 6, Akureyri, www.rub23.is/en. If you like to play with your food, this polished fish restaurant is the place for you. First choose your trout (or lamb, chicken or beef), pick one of the 11 'rubs' as a marinade, then wait for the chef to cook your special combination. There's also a sushi selection, and a recommended tasting menu. **$$$**

Strikið Skipagata 14, Akureyri, www.strikid.is. It looks like an office block from the outside, but this good-quality restaurant in the heart of Akureyri has unsurpassed views of the fjord and mountains from its fifth-floor location. The restaurant serves burgers, pizzas, meat and fish dishes. **$$$**

West and Northwest

Búðarklettur Brákarbraut 13-15, Borgarnes, www.landnam.is/eng/restaurant. The Settlement Centre's restaurant serves hearty pasta, fish and meat mains. Many have a traditional slant – think smoked lamb and herring on rye bread – and there's a large vegetarian selection. **$$**

Café Riis Hafnarbraut 39, Holmavík, www.caferiis.is. A tasteful café/bar/restaurant with pizzas, burgers, freshly caught fish, and Icelandic dishes such as puffin breast with blueberries or smoked lumpfish. Open in summer. **$$**

Hótel Buðir Restaurant Main Road, Buðir, 356 Snæfellsbær; www.hotelbudir.is. Reopened after a devastating fire, this is one of Iceland's finest hotels. Seafood and game predominate in its oceanfront restaurant, including honey-glazed catfish with ginger, chilli and liquorice sauce. **$$$$**

Hótel Flókalundur Vatnsfjörður, 451 Patreksfjörður; www.flokalundur.is. This is the only restaurant in the vicinity. Rosemary-roasted trout, roast lamb and garlic lobster are some of the evening meals served. Also a popular coffee stop for people waiting for the ferry to Snæfellsnes. **$$$**

Logn Hótel Ísafjörður, Silfurtorgi 2, Ísafjörður, www.isafjordurhotels.is/Logn. The most upmarket place in town to eat, with excellent fish dishes and superb views of the fjord. **$$$**

Núpur Guesthouse Dýrafjörður, Þingeyri district, tel: 456 8235. A small, but select evening menu is served (7–9pm) in summer. Fish takes pride of place, along with the restaurant's speciality, goat meat. **$$$**

Travel essentials

Practical information

Accessible Travel

Iceland's association with outdoor activities, combined with its wild volcanic and glacial landscapes, mean that it presents challenges for travellers with disabilities – but progress is being made. Launched in 2022, the Gott aðgengi í ferðaþjónustu (Good Access in Tourism) campaign asks restaurants, hotels, museums and tour operators to display green badges reflecting their accessibility for travellers in wheelchairs, those who are visually impaired, and those who are deaf or hard of hearing. The Ramping Up Iceland campaign has seen most of the businesses on Laugavegur, Reykjavík's main shopping street, become wheelchair-accessible, while the city's buses are following suit. All buildings built after 2012 are required by law to have elevators and accessible bathrooms.

Outside the capital, things can be more challenging, but help is at hand in the form of fantastic tour operator Iceland Unlimited (https://icelandunlimited.is), who run tours all across the country specifically designed to cater for travellers with disabilities.

Accommodation

The Icelandic Tourist Board (www.visiticeland.com) operates a (voluntary) classification system for accommodation, which grades hotels from five stars, for those with the best facilities, down to one star, for the most basic.

Both in Reykjavík and elsewhere in the country, many of the higher-rated hotels are large and impersonal. The capital has some quality hotels with character, and there are one or two elsewhere in the country, but these are the exception. Overall, Icelandic hotels can be quite spartan; and all Icelandic buildings have thin walls and curtains – light sleepers should bring earplugs and an eye mask. In summer, 11 of Iceland's schools, universities and conference centres open as 'summer hotels' (e.g. www.studenthostel.is in Reykjavik). If you are doing a lot of walking or horse riding check if the hotel has a sauna, hot-tub or pool, all of which will be geothermally heated.

There are guesthouses everywhere in Iceland and these are generally welcoming and considerably cheaper than hotels. They vary in quality, but are invariably clean and well-kept. Bathrooms are very often shared. Farmhouse accommodation is also available. More than 170 farms operate through Hey Iceland (www.heyiceland.is).

If you are travelling around, the location of a hotel will probably be more important to you than its facilities. Local tourist offices (see page 140) have comprehensive lists of nearby hotels and staff who can speak English and make reservations for you. If you are travelling between May and September you are advised to book ahead.

Airports

99.9 percent of international flights arrive at **Keflavík International Airport** (www.isavia.is/en/keflavik-airport), 50km (31 miles) from Reykjavík. After every flight arrival, the Flybus (www.re.is/flybus) transfer coach transports passengers to the BSÍ bus terminal about 1.5km (1 mile) from the centre of Reykjavík. The journey takes about 45 minutes and costs about ISK4,500: buy tickets from the ticket machine or ticket booth next to the airport exit. Grayline (https://grayline.is/airport-bus-transfer) runs between the airport and more than 160 drop off points (door-to-door service), including the Reykjavik bus terminal. Taxis from the airport to central Reykjavík will take 30–45 minutes and will cost approximately ISK22,000.

From mid-May to September, some charter flights use Akureyri airport, located around 3km (1.86 miles) south of town. There are also seasonal flights to Greenland from Akureyri.

Reykjavík's Domestic Airport (www.innanlandsflugvellir.is/en/reykjavik-airport) is at the other end of the runway from the Icelandair Hotel Reykjavík Natura, and there are regular buses to and from the city centre. **Myflug Air** (www.myflug.is/en) offers scheduled services to most parts of the country.

Apps

Safe Travel – This app contains up-to-date information on weather and road closures, and allows you to officially log your journeys ahead of setting off. Essential for winter travel and anyone heading to the Interior.

Kringum – Brings locations across Iceland to life with folk tales, historical information and tips for things to see and do – all completely free of charge.

My Aurora Forecast – Handy for aurora hunters trying to figure out whether it's worth heading off on a Northern Lights tour, which can be costly, time consuming and dispiriting if the weather doesn't play ball.

AllTrails – The mother of all hiking apps is as useful in Iceland as it is across the world, with thousands of reliably mapped walking routes, complete with user reviews and listings of points of interest.

Bicycle Rental

Some places around Iceland hire out bikes; make enquiries at tourist offices, hotels and campsites. Cycling is popular around Lake Mývatn: Hotel Reynihlíð and the Hlíð and Bjarg campsites have a reasonable selection. **Reykjavík Bike Tours** (101 Reykjavík, http://icelandbike.com) have rentals and tours.

Budgeting for Your Trip

Following the 2008 financial crisis, Iceland went from being eye-wateringly expensive to merely expensive for foreign visitors.

Getting to Iceland. The main airline serving Iceland is Icelandair, operating from both Europe and North America. Budget airlines PLAY (www.flyplay.com), Wizz Air (https://wizzair.com), Vueling (www.vueling.com), and easyJet (www.easyjet.com) have slightly cheaper flights from various European cities. In summer it is essential to book well in advance to secure the lowest fares. In the UK, Icelandair have fares from London Gatwick, London Heathrow, Manchester and Glasgow.

Accommodation. Top summer prices in Reykjavík are over ISK40,000 for a twin room in a luxury hotel, with en-suite shower or bath, and breakfast included. Guesthouses charge from ISK25,000. Out of season, prices can drop by around 40 percent. In some places you pay about half the price if you use your own sleeping-bag.

Meals. A sit-down lunch in a restaurant costs from ISK1,800 (but look out for cheap lunchtime buffet deals), and dinner from ISK3,000. Alcohol is expensive, with a glass of beer in a restaurant costing around ISK1,000 and a bottle of wine upwards of ISK6,000.

Local transport. Reykjavík's city bus service is good value, with bus tickets costing ISK670. Taxis are costly – the meter starts running as soon as the vehicle pulls up to your hotel, and a trip from Reykjavík to the international airport costs around ISK22,000 (compared to the Flybus ticket price of ISK3,999). In summer, the Highland Bus offers a convenient, hop-on hop-off way to explore the country's more remote interior; passes are available at www.re.is/highland-bus.

Generally, if you visit during the summer, stay in decent hotels, eat out in restaurants most nights and undertake a few activities, you should expect to pay upwards of ISK35,000 per person per day, based on two people sharing. However, it is possible to cut costs by staying in guesthouses or youth hostels and eating the odd meal in a restaurant – for this, you should reckon on about ISK25,000 per day. Camping and self-catering will cost around ISK12,500 per day.

Domestic flights can be cheaper than buses: so-called 'net offers' are available on most Air Iceland flights, which when booked in advance help to secure the best price for any particular flight.

Camping

There are around 70 registered campsites in Iceland, although you can camp almost anywhere if you get the landowners' permission. Within national parks and conservation areas, camping is only allowed at designated spots. Official campsites are found in most towns and villages, at national parks, conservation areas, places of natural beauty and some farms and community centres. The standard varies. Expect to pay from ISK1800 per person per night for anything from a layer of pumice and an earth closet, to soft turf and hot showers. The recognised sites are open from mid-May or June to August or mid-September.

The Iceland Tourist Board (www.visiticeland.com) has camping listings on its website. Easy equipment hire is available in Reykjavík from companies such as Iceland Camping Equipment, (www.iceland-camping-equipment.com, Klapparstígur 16).

Car Hire (See also Driving and Budgeting for your Trip)

Several major international rental companies are represented in Iceland, as well as locally based firms. Prices are high. You must be at least 21 years old to hire a car in Iceland. Insurance is compulsory and not always included in the quoted price, so check first.

The following companies offer a full range of vehicles: Hertz (www.hertz.is), Europcar (www.europcar.is), Avis (www.avis.is), Iceland Car Rental (www.icelandcarrental.is). Many hire companies offer one-way rentals, allowing you to drive from Reykjavík to Akureyri, for example, and then return by air.

It is worthwhile going over your intended route with the rental company to check what roads are allowed for your type of vehicle. Note that insurance companies will not cover hire cars taken into the interior or on F-roads.

Climate

Influenced by the warm Gulf Stream and prevailing southwesterly winds, Iceland's temperate oceanic climate is surprisingly mild for the latitude. However, summers are generally cool, and the country is often wet and windy, with the weather changing dramatically from day to day, or even hourly. Basically, it's sensible to be prepared for all eventualities. The weather is drier and sunnier in the north and east than the south and west, although no less windy. The south coast is notoriously wet.

You can get weather information in English by calling tel: 902 0600 or visiting www.vedur.is/english.

Average rainfall and temperatures:

	J	F	M	A	M	J	J	A	S	O	N	D
ºC												
min	-2	-2	1	1	4	7	9	8	6	3	0	-2
max	2	3	4	6	10	12	14	14	11	7	4	2
Rainfall												
mm	76	72	82	58	44	50	52	62	66	85	72	79

Crime and Safety (See also Emergencies and Police)

Iceland is an extremely peaceful and law-abiding nation. Of the few people in prison, most are drugs offenders. Public places are well lit. Violent crime is virtually non-existent, bar the odd domestic dispute and drunken brawl. The latter is most likely on Friday and Saturday nights, when the city's youth takes to the streets of central Reykjavík on a (mostly good-humoured) drunken spree.

Driving

Despite the high cost of car hire, rental may provide the only way to see everything you wish in the time available. Driving in Iceland can also be a real pleasure – the roads are not busy and the freedom to stop to admire the scenery or go for a walk is a huge bonus. Be prepared for journeys to take a lot longer than you might expect from the distances involved.

Road conditions. While much of the main highway encircling the country is surfaced, many routes in Iceland are just gravel or unmade and full of potholes. Some roads are prone to flooding, and bridges are often single-lane. Livestock make frequent mad dashes into the middle of the road.

Sandstorms can be a hazard along the coast and in some parts of the interior. In winter, snow and ice are common, and studded snow tyres are essential. For information on road conditions call tel: 1777 or check on www.vegagerdin.is.

Rules and regulations. Icelanders drive on the right. The speed limit is 50kmh (30mph) in urban areas, 80kmh (50mph) on gravel roads in rural areas and 90kmh (55mph) on asphalt roads out of the towns.

Driving off roads is illegal (fines are extremely high), seat belts are compulsory in the front and back of a car, and headlights must be used at all times, day and night. Drink-driving is taken very seriously by the authorities – it is against the law to drive a vehicle in Iceland after consuming any alcohol. Offenders lose their licences and face heavy fines. Mobile phones must be used with a hands-free set while driving.

Fuel. In Reykjavík there are several 24-hour filling stations. Those that close overnight usually have automatic pumps that take banknotes or credit cards (but check that yours works while the kiosk is still manned!). Around the ring road there are filling stations every 50km (30 miles) or so, but if in doubt fill up before you move on.

Parking. Reykjavík has plenty of parking meters, ticket machines and car parks, some of which are covered and attended. On-street parking can be hard to find. Elsewhere in the country you will encounter few problems, and there are large free car parks at most of the major tourist sites.

Road signs. The usual international symbols are used on road signs, but look out also for:

Einbreið brú Single-lane bridge (often marked by flashing orange lights)
Malbik endar Unmade road
Blindhæð Blind summit

Help and information. Tourist boards have leaflets about driving on unmade roads and in winter, as well as lists of all road signs. Also see the website www.safetravel.is.

Electricity

The electric current in Iceland is 220 volts, 50 Hz AC. Plugs are European round pin with two prongs.

Embassies and Consulates

Ireland: Honorary Consul in Reykjavík, Mr Jens Þórðarson tel: 840 7134, jens.thordarson@honoraryconsul.ie

United Kingdom: Laufásvegur 31, 101 Reykjavík, tel: 550 5100, www.gov.uk/government/world/organisations/british-embassy-reykjavik

United States: Engjateigur 7, 105 Reykjavík, tel: 595 2200, https://is.usembassy.gov

The Icelandic Foreign Ministry has a full list of diplomatic representatives on its website: www.mfa.is.

Emergencies (See also Health and Medical Care)

To contact the police, ambulance, fire service or other emergency situations, tel: **112**.

In case of serious illness or accidents, there is a 24-hour casualty department in Landspítali University Hospital (Fossvogur, tel: 543 1000, www.landspitali.is).

Chemists are signed *Apótek*, and there is at least one in every town. Lyfja (Lágmúli 5, Reykjavík, tel: 533 2300) is open daily from 8am–midnight.

In case of dental emergencies, www.tannlaeknavaktin.is, tel: 426 8000.

LGBTQ+ Travel

Iceland has a tolerant attitude towards LGBTQ+ people. The country had the world's first openly gay prime minister, and passed a gender-neutral marriage bill in 2010.

For information and advice contact: The National Queer Organisation of Iceland/Samtökin '78, 4th Floor, Suðurgata 3, 101 Reykjavík, www.samtokin78.is.

There is an annual Gay Pride celebration in Reykjavík every August, www.facebook.com/reykjavikpride/. More information about the gay scene in Iceland can be found at www.gayice.is.

Getting There (See also Airports and Budgeting)

The fastest and cheapest way to get to Iceland is by air. **Icelandair** (www.icelandair.com) is the main airline serving Iceland, operating from both Europe and North America. In the UK, Icelandair serves London Gatwick, London Heathrow, Manchester and Glasgow. In North America; Anchorage, Boston, Chicago, Denver, Minneapolis, New York, Orlando, Seattle, Toronto, Vancouver (seasonal) and Washington, among others.

Budget airline **Wizz Air** (www.wizzair.com) has daily year-round departures from London Luton.

Jet2.com flies seasonally from Birmingham, East Midlands, Glasgow, Leeds, London, Manchester, and Newcastle.

easyJet (www.easyjet.com) has year-round departures from London

Luton, Bristol, Edinburgh and Manchester.

The Faroese company, **Smyril Line** www.smyrilline.com, operates a weekly (twice a week in summer) ferry service to Iceland. The ship Norrøna sails from Hirtshals in Denmark to Seyðisfjörður in eastern Iceland, calling in at Tórshavn (Faroe Islands).

Guides and Tours (See also Public Transport)

One of the best ways of seeing the main sites is by organised coach tours. The drivers and tour leaders are always well informed and speak English. If you want to travel into the interior or onto glaciers, a tour is often the only choice.

Tours are well run, and many allow you to do some exploring by yourself. **Reykjavík Excursions** (BSI Bus Terminal, 101 Reykjavík, www.re.is) are the biggest providers of day tours from Reykjavík to the west and southwest of the country, including whale-watching, the Blue Lagoon and glacier tours.

Tours can last from half a day to three weeks. As well as sightseeing there are tours specialising in hiking, geology, birdwatching, fishing and horse riding. Sports-orientated tours have good-quality equipment and guides who are fully trained for the environment. For full details, contact the Icelandic Tourist Office (www.visiticeland.com).

Health and Medical Care (See also Emergencies)

Iceland is one of the world's healthiest nations, with low pollution and bountiful clean air. Food is usually fresh and organic, and the water is clean to drink, although you should never drink from glacial rivers or streams.

The standard of medical care is very high, but nonetheless, all visitors should have adequate medical insurance, though an agreement exists between Iceland, the UK and Scandinavian countries for limited health insurance coverage of its residents. Travellers from those countries should obtain the European Health Insurance Card (EHIC) before leaving home, or a UK Global Health Insurance Card (GHIC) card if you are from the UK.

Despite the high latitude, the Icelandic sun can still burn, especially when reflected off snow and ice. Sunblock and good sunglasses should be worn if you are outside for long periods. The summer can bring airborne pollen from birch and grass, so carry hay fever tablets if you suffer.

In extreme circumstances hypothermia is a possibility. Symptoms include shivering, numbness, dizzy spells and confused behaviour. If affected, take shelter, remove and replace wet clothing, and consume hot drinks and high-calorie food.

Every year all too many visitors are injured, sometimes seriously, by putting feet or hands into boiling hot mud pools and springs, so take care to avoid this. If you are planning to take part in any unusual or 'dangerous' sports, make sure that these are covered by your policy.

Language

Icelandic is a Germanic language and has barely changed since Viking times. Although it is grammatically complex, anyone who speaks one of the other Scandinavian languages or German will recognise words and features. Thankfully, though, there is no need to master Icelandic to enjoy a holiday in Iceland, since nearly all Icelanders speak excellent English, particularly the young.

yes **já**
no **nei**
hello/hi **halló/hæ**
good morning/afternoon **góðan dáginn**
good evening **gott kvöld**
good night **góða nótt**
goodbye **bless**
How do you do? **Sæll** (to a man); **sæl** (to a woman)
Fine, thanks. **Mél liður vel, takk.**
thank you **takk fyrir**
yesterday/today/tomorrow **í gær/í dag/á morgun**
Where/when/how? **Hvar/hvenær/hvernig?**

How long/how far? **Hvað lengi/hversu langt?**
left/right **vinstri/hægri**
hot/cold **heitt/kalt**
old/new **gamalt/ungt**
open/closed **opið/lokað**
vacant/occupied **laus/upptekinn**
early/late **snemma/seint**

Money (See also Budgeting for your Trip)

The Icelandic currency is the króna (ISK; plural: krónur), divided into 100 aurar. Notes are in denominations of ISK5,000, 2,000, 1,000 and 500, coins in denominations of ISK100, 50, 10, 5 and 1.

Currency Exchange. Banks will change foreign currency or travellers cheques – US dollars, sterling and euros are all easily exchanged. Outside normal banking hours you can exchange money at major hotels. There are 24-hour exchange facilities available at Keflavík Airport: look for **Landsbankinn** in the arrival hall for arriving passengers; on the second level for departing passengers.

Credit Cards. Credit cards are used everywhere in Iceland, with the most ubiquitous being Visa and MasterCard/EuroPay. American Express, JCB and Diners are far less common. Choosing to pay in krona rather than pounds, when prompted, can avoid extra charges.

Cash advances are available on Visa and MasterCard/EuroPay from all banks, savings banks and automatic cash machines.

ATMs. The simplest way to obtain Icelandic krónur is from an ATM cash machine – plentiful in Reykjavík and other Icelandic towns. There are cash machines at the airport and at many banks. The charges will depend on your bank, but the rate of exchange is generally better than any other method.

Travellers Cheques. Hotels will exchange travellers cheques and banknotes for guests, at a rate slightly below the bank rate, depending on the availability of cash in the till.

Opening Times

Museums and attractions are generally open from 10am–5pm. Shops, banks and other services rarely close for lunch. The following are rough guides to opening times in Reykjavík; opening times elsewhere in the country are usually shorter than this.

Banks: Mon–Fri 9.15am–4pm.

Post Offices: Mon–Fri 9am–6pm.

Shops: Mon–Fri 9am–6pm, Sat 10am–1pm/2pm/3pm/4pm. Smaller shops may not open until 10am. Some supermarkets open until 11pm daily.

Liquor Stores: Reykjavík: Mon–Thurs 11am–6pm, Fri 11am–7pm, Sat 11am–6pm. Other stores usually much shorter hours – see www.vinbudin.is for details.

Police

In such a law-abiding country the police keep a low profile, and you are unlikely to come across them unless you commit a motoring offence. They can normally speak some English.

Police Emergency Number, tel: 112.

Reykjavík Police Headquarters is at Hverfisgata 113–115, tel: 444 1000. The Reykjavík city-centre police station is at Tryggvagata 19, tel: 569 9025. For lost property, contact the police, tel: 444 2500.

Public Holidays

The following are public holidays in Iceland. Note that most businesses, banks and shops will be closed on these days, and public transport will be more limited than usual.

Fixed dates:

1 January New Year's Day

1 May Labour Day

17 June National Day

24 December Christmas Eve (from noon)

25 December Christmas Day

26 December Boxing Day
31 December New Year's Eve (from noon)

Movable dates:

Maundy Thursday
Good Friday
Easter Sunday
Easter Monday
First day of summer (first Thursday after 18 April)
Ascension Day
Whit Sunday
Whit Monday
Bank Holiday Monday (first Monday in August)

Telephones

The code for Iceland is +354, followed by a seven-digit number. There are no area codes. To call abroad from Iceland, dial 00, plus the country code.

Payphones are becoming rare, but can still be found in post offices, petrol stations, swimming pools, shopping malls and transport hubs. These take coins or phone cards, which can be bought at kiosks or post offices in various denominations.

The four main mobile operators in Iceland are Siminn, Vodafone, and Nova. Pre-paid SIM cards can be bought at filling stations.

Useful numbers are as follows:
1811: international directory enquiries
118: national directory assistance

Time Zones

Iceland is on GMT all year round. Time in summer is as below.

Los Angeles	Chicago	New York	**Iceland**	London	Sydney
5am	7am	8am	**noon**	1pm	10pm

Tipping

Service is always included in the bill, so tipping is not normally required. It is not usual to tip taxi drivers.

Toilets

Public toilets are a rarity: there is one on Ingólfstorg (close to the tourist office); one at the top of Frakkastígur (close to Hallgrímskirkja); one on Vegamótastígur; and one at the end of Lækjargata (near the northeast corner of Tjörnin). It is better to make use of the facilities at your accommodation or at a bar or café.

Tourist Information

The tourist information structure in Iceland is a little complex. The Icelandic Tourist Board (Geirsgata 9, Reykjavík 101, www.ferdamalastofa.is/en) promotes Iceland abroad. The regional Tourist Information Centres are separately run, and some parts of the country also have Marketing Agencies. Staff speak excellent English and are usually very helpful. Opening times vary, but in summer they open early and close around 7pm.

The Tourist Information Centre in Reykjavík is at the City Hall, Tjarnargata 11, www.visitreykjavik.is.

In Akureyri, the information centre has closed. However, you can still find information at www.visitakureyri.is. Brochures and maps are available at the Akureyri Thermal Pool, Municipal Library, and at the Akureyri Art Museum.

Information can be obtained worldwide from www.visiticeland.com.

Transport

Buses. There is an excellent system of buses both in Reykjavík (run by the Reykjavík bus company Strætó) and across the country. In the capital there are two terminals for the yellow city buses, one near the harbour at Lækjartorg, at the junction of Lækjargata and Austurstræti, the other at Hlemmur, at the far end of the main shopping street, Laugavegur. Maps showing all the routes are available from terminals, tourist offices, and at www.straeto.is.

Most buses now accept contactless card payment. If you are changing buses ask for a *skiftimiði*, which is valid on all buses for around 75 minutes. The Reykjavík City Card (see page 39) offers free unlimited travel for 24, 48 or 72 hours.

Long-distance buses operate from the BSÍ Coach Terminal, Vatnsmýrarvegur (www.bsi.is). There are a variety of 'bus passports' available if you are going to use the bus network extensively, and they come with different time limits.

Taxis. Taxis are available in all the major towns. There are ranks in Reykjavík on Lækjargata and Eiríksgata. To order a cab by phone call: Borgarbílastöðin (www.borgarbilastodin.is), tel: 552 2440; BSR (https://bsr.is), tel: 561 0000; or Hreyfill-Bæjarleiðir (www.hreyfill.is), tel: 588 5522.

Ferries. The ferry Herjólfur runs to the Westman Islands (tel: 481 2800, www.herjolfur.is), from Landeyjahöfn near Hvollsvöllur on the south coast, or from Þorlákshöfn in bad weather – check sailings before travel. Sæferðir (Smiðjustígur 3, 340 Stykkisholmur 3, www.seatours.is) runs the ferry Baldur, which sails to the West Fjords, as well as whale-watching tours and other excursions. *Sæfari* sails from Dalvík to Grímsey (via Hrisey) in the summer (Samskip, Ranarbraut 2b, 620 Dalvík, www.samskip.is).

Train Travel. There are no trains in Iceland.

Visas and Entry Requirements

Iceland is a signatory to the Schengen Agreement, so, in principle, residents of other Schengen countries (Norway plus all EU countries except Ireland) can enter the country with national identity cards rather than passports. Flights from the UK go through passport control. UK citizens don't need a visa to visit Iceland if the visit is less than 90 days; if it is more than 90 days, travellers need to check with the Icelandic Directorate of Immigration (www.utl.is/index.php?lang=en) to find out what type of visa or permit you may need. Iceland doesn't require visas from citizens of EU states, the US, Canada, Australia or New Zealand; South African citizens do require one. The normal entry stamp in your passport is valid for a stay of up to three months, and your passport must be valid for a further three months beyond your proposed departure date. There are no currency restrictions.

Index

MINI
ICELAND

Second Edition 2025

Editor: Siobhan Warwicker
Author: Daniel Stables
Picture Editor: Piotr Kala
Picture Manager: Tom Smyth
Cartography Update: Katie Bennett
Layout: Grzegorz Madejak
Production Operations Manager: Katie Bennett
Publishing Technology Manager: Rebeka Davies
Head of Publishing: Sarah Clark
Photography Credits: All images Shutterstock except: Dreamstime 72, 77, 79, 97, 98; Fotolia 82; iStock 15CL, 55, 65, 67, 68, 107; Ming Tang-Evans/ Apa Publications 9, 16TL, 23, 29, 34, 35, 36, 40, 43, 44, 57, 61, 69, 70, 73, 75, 80, 83, 86, 89, 90, 92, 94, 100, 108, 113, 115, 117
Cover Credits: The Black Church of Budir **SandaloFilms/Shutterstock**

About the author
Daniel Stables is a travel writer based in Manchester, UK. He writes travel articles for National Geographic and the BBC, and his debut narrative travel book, *Fiesta: A Journey Through Festivity* is coming out in early 2026. He also hosts a podcast, Hungry Ghosts, about food and travel. You can find his work on X @DanStables, Instagram @DanStabs, or at danielstables.co.uk.

Distribution
UK, Ireland and Europe: Apa Publications (UK) Ltd; mail@roughguides.com
United States and Canada: Two Rivers; ips@ingramcontent.com
Australia and New Zealand: Woodslane; info@woodslane.com.au
Worldwide: Apa Publications (UK) Ltd; mail@roughguides.com

MIX
Paper from responsible sources
FSC® C014138

Special Sales, Content Licensing and CoPublishing
Rough Guides can be purchased in bulk quantities at discounted prices. We can create special editions, personalized jackets and corporate imprints tailored to your needs. mail@roughguides.com

roughguides.com

EU Representative
LOGOS EUROPE, 9 rue Nicolas Poussin, 17000, LA ROCHELLE, France; Contact@logoseurope.eu; +33 (0) 667937378

Printed by Finidr in Czech Republic

ISBN: 9781835292310

This book was produced using **Typefi** automated publishing software.

A catalogue record for this book is available from the British Library

Contact us
Every effort has been made to ensure that this publication is accurate, free from safety risks, and provides accurate information. However, changes and errors are inevitable. The publisher is not responsible for any resulting loss, inconvenience, injury or safety concerns arising from the use of this book. If you notice any errors, outdated information, or potential safety risks, please send your comments with the subject line "Rough Guide Mini Iceland Update" to mail@roughguides.com.